The Holy Crap Cookbook

The
Holy
Crap
Cookbook

CORIN MULLINS
with CLAUDIA HOWARD

 WONDERFULLY HEALTHY, MARVELLOUSLY DELICIOUS
AND FANTASTICALLY EASY GLUTEN-FREE RECIPES

Douglas & McIntyre

DOUGLAS & MCINTYRE (2013) LTD.
PO Box 219 Madeira Park, B.C., V0N 2H0
www.douglas-mcintyre.com

EDITED by Lucy Kenward
INDEX by Nicola Goshulak
COVER AND TEXT DESIGN by Diane Robertson
COVER AND INTERIOR PHOTOGRAPHY by Christina Symons except where
   otherwise noted

Printed and bound in Canada
Distributed in the U.S. by Publishers Group West

DOUGLAS AND MCINTYRE (2013) LTD. acknowledges the support of the Canada Council for the Arts, which last year invested $153 million to bring the arts to Canadians throughout the country. We also gratefully acknowledge financial support from the Government of Canada through the Canada Book Fund and from the Province of British Columbia through the BC Arts Council and the Book Publishing Tax Credit.

CATALOGUING DATA AVAILABLE FROM LIBRARY AND ARCHIVES CANADA
Library and Archives Canada Cataloguing in Publication

Mullins, Corin, author
   Holy crap cookbook : sixty wonderfully healthy, marvellously delicious and fantastically easy gluten-free recipes / Corin Mullins, with Claudia Howard.

Includes bibliographical references and index.

Issued in print and electronic formats.

ISBN 978-1-77162-139-7 (paperback).--ISBN 978-1-77162-140-3 (html)

   1. Gluten-free diet--Recipes. 2. Cookbooks. I. Howard, Claudia, 1957-, author II. Title.

RM237.86.M84 2016   641.5'639311   C2016-905093-9
                                       C2016-905094-7

THIS COOKBOOK is dedicated to everyone who believes a healthy lifestyle is just as much about laughing out loud as it is about making nutritious food choices (most of the time).
—Brian and Corin Mullins

CONTENTS

INTRODUCTION

Holy Crap

Yes, that is the name of our amazing cereal. And these two expressive words are also just right to describe the remarkable journey we've had since developing this delicious, profoundly nourishing superfood that's so easy to eat anytime, anywhere.

And, Holy Crap, *What* a Journey It's Been

It all started in a very small way. Seven years ago—with expectations of nothing more than a good breakfast—I decided to direct my passion for preparing good food toward creating a simple and wholesome cereal mix for my husband, Brian.

Back then, in an effort to be healthier, Brian was eating bran cereal with raisins every morning, but food sensitivities were giving him allergic reactions, with even the dust from the flakes causing him to cough. We reviewed the other breakfast options lined from floor to ceiling in the cereal aisle, but virtually every one of them was loaded with wheat, sugar, salt and a disconcerting list of chemicals with unpronounceable names. Despite all these choices stacked up in front of us, *not one* looked very good.

> I've always said you're only as healthy as the air you breathe, the water you drink and the food you eat.

I believed there should be a better option, so I went straight to my kitchen to make something from scratch. Using only the healthiest organic ingredients I could source, and fast-forwarding through 21 recipe attempts, I felt I had finally got it just right.

(CLOCKWISE FROM UPPER LEFT) Brian and Corin Mullins cut the ribbon in front of the new Holy Crap factory in Gibsons, BC, October 4, 2011—*Claudia Howard photo*. Corin Mullins at the Granville Street Market, Vancouver, BC, February 2010—*Courtesy of Corin Mullins*. Single serve Holy Crap cereal packaged by NASA for Commander Chris Hadfield's mission aboard the International Space Station—*Chris Hadfield photo*. First Nations singers Christine McLellan and Terry Aleck performing ceremonial blessing at the Holy Crap Factory opening in Gibsons, BC, October 4, 2011—*Chris Mortensen photo*. Corin Mullins shows assorted parfaits made from one bag of Holy Crap cereal—*Claudia Howard photo*. Brian and Corin Mullins pictured in the Holy Crap factory—*Claudia Howard photo*. Brian and Corin Mullins on the *Dragons' Den* set, CBC, Toronto, May 2011—*Courtesy of CBC*. (CENTRE) Product packaging created by Sechelt-based graphic designer Karen Weissenborn—*Courtesy of HapiFoods Group Inc.*

Instead of chemicals, my homemade mix was made from real food. Instead of more ingredients, it had fewer . . . but the nourishment in each of these carefully chosen elements was astounding and, nutritionally, far surpassing anything Brian had eaten before. Instead of worrisome additives, this cereal contained only pure food from certified organic farmers. And, best of all, it was delicious and could be prepared in seconds with just a little water. It could be enjoyed cold or warm—with absolutely no cooking required.

Brian loved my homemade cereal and, as an added bonus, once he started eating it every morning he had more energy and endurance. We were so happy with these results that I decided to go for the gusto and package some up to offer for sale in our community.

At that time, Brian and I had just moved to the community of Sechelt, on British Columbia's spectacular Sunshine Coast, to look after my mom. We had relocated from Sidney, BC, following my retirement from Air Canada after a 30-year career as a flight attendant; however, at 58 I wasn't ready to stop working yet.

There were few jobs in Sechelt and although I found a couple of part-time positions, Brian and I decided we wanted to invest a little money and a lot of "sweat equity" into making our lives better by growing our own small business. Along the way, we created many jobs within our local community, a whole new category in the grocery aisle and a multi-million-dollar global company.

After investing the grand sum of $129 into packaging and preparation, I set up a table among Sechelt's farmers and artisans at the weekend market and was very proud to sell the first 10 bags of "Hapi Food cereal." A couple of days later, one very excited customer called me at home to say, "*Holy crap*, this *really* works—it's amazing!" Brian, with his strong marketing background, immediately responded, "Let's call it 'Holy Crap!'"

My initial reaction was "No way! How can I sell something called Holy **Crap**?" Still, I agreed to keep an open mind . . . along with my sense of fun.

We talked over the name with Karen Weissenborn, our neighbour in Sechelt and the graphic designer of our package labels, and she suggested that at the next farmers' market we label half of the bags Hapi Food and the other half Holy Crap to test what sold better. I'm guessing you have a pretty good idea of how that went. That Saturday, I sold just two bags of Hapi

Food and *more than a hundred of Holy Crap!* When I arrived home, I said to Brian, "*Holy Crap,* this isn't such a bad name after all!"

One day that same summer, we arrived home from the market to find a woman waiting at our doorstep. In tears, she said she was overwhelmed with gratitude and had come to thank us personally: her daughter suffered with an eating disorder but was now, miraculously, eating our cereal. This story—along with thousands more we would go on to hear—taught us that we are actually in the business of well-being. And this is what energized me through all the challenges ahead.

As the Sechelt Farmers' & Artisans' Market came to a close at the end of the summer, we arranged for a kiosk at Vancouver's indoor Granville Island Public Market. This meant getting up on Saturdays and Sundays at 4:30 am to be on the 6:20 ferry. Our weekdays were spent madly making cereal and packaging it up one bag at a time. It was both an exhausting and exciting time: not only was Holy Crap being well received by Granville Island's traditional weekend shoppers, but it was attracting steady new interest of a more global nature.

Our winter at the Granville Market coincided with the 2010 Winter Olympics in Vancouver. Athletes and coaches were stopping by to check out the health benefits and nutritional profile of Holy Crap. Some—like one gentleman who slipped back three times in one morning for product samples I was offering—were buying it by the case. Visitors from around the world, in town for the big event, were picking up bags of Holy Crap, frequently because they were tickled by its name, and reordering it through our website when they arrived at home.

People were buying Holy Crap for a laugh because of its name. But then they would start eating it . . . and they loved its taste and consistency, loved that they were more regular and felt better, and loved that their food cravings were reduced and they had more energy. They were buying Holy Crap for its name but coming back for more because they loved what the cereal was doing for them.

Holy Crap, We're on *Dragons' Den*

Energized by the excitement our cereal was creating, we started thinking about ways to reach more people—and, for a second time, Brian's marketing instincts had bigger-than-life results.

One of his favourite shows, CBC's *Dragons' Den*, where aspiring Canadian entrepreneurs pitch business deals to a panel of venture capitalists, was auditioning in Vancouver. Thinking it would be good publicity—but never dreaming we'd get a deal—Brian suggested we give it a shot. We made it through the audition and were invited to make an appearance in November 2010, where we proposed selling 20 percent of our new company for $120,000. In the fastest deal ever made on the show—even to this day—Jim Treliving of Boston Pizza fame tasted Holy Crap and exclaimed, "I love it. I want to buy it!"

But the story doesn't end there. The evening the show aired, we received so many orders for Holy Crap that the net worth of our company (called Hapi Foods after the original 10 bags sold) tripled to $1.5 million overnight.

More than 10,000 orders from all over North America came roaring in that one night, causing a PayPal representative to call us in a panic to ask if there was some kind of racket going on—and when we described what we were selling, he bought some himself! That night we set a PayPal record for the highest volume ever processed in Canada.

I hired eight employees the next day—all family and friends—and scrambled to get enough ingredients and supplies to fill all the orders. We had to buy more printers, borrow money to pay more than $200,000 in postage, and expand our workspace fast!

It no longer made sense to sell a fifth of our company for $120,000. Yet, despite this, Jim Treliving has graciously mentored us since that night on *Dragons' Den* and still reminds us that he eats Holy Crap every single morning.

A follow-up on CBC in 2012 declared Holy Crap to be the most successful business to ever come out of the *Dragons' Den*. And to this day, reruns of the show aired internationally attract people from around the world to order our cereal from holycrap.com.

We were invited back to *Dragons' Den* in 2015, but again we passed on finalizing any deals despite some good offers. The reason? New investment hinged on our leaving the Sunshine Coast for Calgary, and we are committed to staying in our local community where Holy Crap makes an important difference to the lives of many employees and their families.

Holy Crap, Local Gone Global

We see keeping things local as a win-win situation: by staying true to our roots on the Sunshine Coast we have bettered our community by providing good jobs and donating tens of thousands of dollars to local charities. And in return, it's the energy of the Coast—our suppliers, local credit union and, most of all, our wonderful staff—that makes our company exceptional. *All* of our cereal is made in the tiny town of Gibsons on the Sunshine Coast in our brand-new certified gluten-free, organic, kosher and nut-free factory.

Our staff are computer-literate, social-networking wizards who are excited to be producing the best cereal on earth. They earn twice the average entry wage and enjoy a health-care plan, flex schedules and a share in our success. Brian and I believe in treating other people the way we wish to be treated, and we want our team to be so happy they never leave. We're proud that we are now welcoming second-generation staff to our Holy Crap family.

> The Holy Crap factory is the world's largest survival kit! The base inventory in our Sunshine Coast facility of 30,000 bags of cereal is available to our isolated community in the event BC Ferries stop running due to any natural disaster. A single 8-ounce (227-gram) package of Holy Crap with water provides nourishment for eight days in the event of an emergency, and is easy to store and lasts for at least 18 months.

Yet despite staying local we have gone viral in the global food revolution: our cereal, originally sold one bag at a time on Saturdays at the Sechelt Farmers' & Artisans' Market, is now distributed to more than 40 countries around the world—and, in addition to providing stellar nutrition to so many people on Earth, has rocketed to the International Space Station.

Holy Crap, Off to the Space Station

In 2011, Grade 4 student Riley Weimer entered the Canadian Space Agency's Snacks for Space contest with this submission: "Holy Crap cereal (this is not a joke)—You add either water or milk or soy milk. It is an awesome, great-tasting, very healthy snack."

The criteria required the snacks to be Canadian made and suitable for cosmic conditions. The food needed to have a long shelf life, be free of dust and crumbs, and be easy to prepare and consume in space. Holy Crap—and Riley—was one of 12 winners!

Canadian astronaut Chris Hadfield met with CSA and NASA nutrition experts to taste food samples and choose his spaceflight menu—and we were dazzled when he picked Holy Crap as part of his five-month interstellar sustenance package.

> While in orbit, Chris Hadfield sent us a photo, along with the out-of-this-world compliment that Holy Crap was the "best taste in space!"

Whether from space or back here on Earth, we frequently hear how delicious our cereal is and how easy it is to eat—although on Expedition 35 it did require an intergalactic NASA packaging treatment. This inspired us to offer single-serve (recyclable) packages of Holy Crap and Holy Crap Plus Gluten Free Oats to Earthlings. These are perfect for tossing into a handbag or backpack for those busy days on the run.

Holy Crap, Seeds of Confrontation

While we sometimes can't help but say *holy crap, look how far we've come*, this doesn't mean it's been a snap . . .

Business is full of sharp elbows, and because Brian and I started out in a brand-new direction in our later fifties, we've had our share of jabs. The food business is tough and we've learned the hard way that success is about perseverance, about sticking to it. Basically, you've got to keep going to remain sane—and as we're fifties' kids who were taught to do that, that's just what we do.

Take our chia misadventure . . . which led to our being threatened and robbed of more than half a million dollars.

> Chia has always had its share of controversy, so perhaps we should have expected a problem. When the Spanish conquered the Aztecs, they torched virtually all of this revered crop field by field; it was more valuable than gold to the Aztecs, being a superfood that could be stored for years as a safeguard against famine.

After our *Dragons' Den*–inspired blast of 10,000 orders in one night, we had to get serious about finding ingredients—and a lot of them. Yet, despite the fact that we made very careful arrangements, our two anticipated 10-tonne shipping containers of precious chia simply did not show up. Our broker just shrugged it off and we had to stop production entirely for two long weeks. While we kept our staff working—painting, installing equipment and hosting in-store demos—it felt like the very future of our company was teetering in the balance. Brian and I agreed to take a more

The chia crop in Morales, Mexico, that was purchased but never delivered—*Cam Watt photo.*

hands-on approach and consider sourcing chia from a co-op in Morales, Mexico. With a collective of 20 farms, it could provide us with 180 tons of chia that would carry us for at least a year and a half. And there would be no middleman; our money would go straight into the hands of hard-working growers.

Having grown up in Valencia, Spain, I speak Spanish. I flew to Mexico to meet with these farmers face to face, and with the help of a lawyer drew up a deal that *seemed* good for all, sealing it with a handshake and a $600,000 deposit. It was an eventful day for us when we sent trucks to San Diego to load up our first delivery—60 tonnes' of freshly harvested chia seeds sent north from Mexico! But then we got a shock: we were curtly informed that the chia was off limits because of paperwork problems. Our trucks literally had to pull away empty while this warehouse was stuffed with our prepaid chia.

After more than 100 frantic calls and emails to the co-op—all ignored—we finally unravelled a bitter truth: the chia that we had handed over hundreds of thousands of dollars for *had been resold to other brokers.*

Brian says I'm a reluctant CEO but that I stick with it because I'm such an advocate of good food. Being bamboozled like this truly did shake my confidence to the core. And, after all our good efforts, this deal gone wrong

made our previous misadventure look like nothing but a hiccup. This time half our year's supply was at risk, our money had been swallowed up and we were scrambling for chia seeds more than ever because sales of Holy Crap cereal were exceeding expectations.

In a scene of bitter irony, I was finally able to track down 20 tons of chia for purchase and when I picked it up and looked at the lot numbers on the bags, I realized I was paying *a second time* for the very same seeds I had originally plunked down money for!

When we demanded that money be returned on our twice-paid chia, we were told, at least loosely interpreted, that we would be the last people ever to be paid if I spoke a single word to anyone else in our industry about what had happened. Instead of making me shrink back though, this bullying made me toughen up.

I believe in standing my ground when wronged and Brian does too. I vowed to never prepay for an ingredient again—and to stick to a payment schedule of 30 days *after* inspection—and I have. Now I always send someone from our company to pick up a large harvest and escort it right from the field to the factory warehouse. And this story hasn't ended yet, as we have a lawyer on the case, a good one who is optimistic we will see our money again. Meanwhile, I continue to share our chia tale with others and, because of this, we have made many new and better buying connections.

When people hear some of our business stories, their first reaction is often, "Wow, it's amazing you two are still married!" Well, we are. Together Brian and I are like a tree; we've got to be able to bend in the wind. We do what needs to be done together and, most of the time, meet halfway. But we also strongly respect each other's opinion, so the bottom line for me is that if Brian disagrees passionately with something it's not done. And if I disagree with something, it's exactly the same.

Persevering—and always having each other's back—is what has got us to where we are now and, despite being a "reluctant CEO," I was honoured to be one of the first two Canadian winners of the EY Entrepreneurial Winning Women award in 2013. I also won a spot in an invitation-only leadership program for businesswomen. Following that, Brian and I were featured on the front page of the business section in The *New York Times*—and that was a thrilling Holy Crap moment for both of us and for everyone sharing our journey.

(TOP ROW) Corin and Brian Mullins at home on the Sunshine Coast, British Columbia.

Holy Crap (BOTTOM LEFT) contains organic chia, organic buckwheat, organic hulled hemp seeds, organic raisins, organic dried cranberries, organic apple bits and organic cinnamon. Skinny B (BOTTOM CENTRE) contains 50 per cent more chia than Holy Crap, along with buckwheat and hemp seeds, all three among the oldest perfect foods know to humans. Holy Crap Plus Gluten Free Oats (BOTTOM RIGHT) contains Holy Crap cereal plus organic gluten free oats and organic maple flakes for a hint of sweetness.

Holy Crap, Superfood Cereal

As our customers have expressed thousands of times: *Holy Crap is amazing stuff,* and experts—from scientists to nutritionists to doctors—agree. All three of our chief ingredients—chia, buckwheat and hulled hemp seeds—are ancient seeds given superfood status for their nutritional oomph and ability to optimize health.

> **"Don't eat this cereal if you don't want to change your life . . ."** —BRIAN MULLINS

Our employees take great pride every day in ensuring the quality of our product—and every single one of them takes Holy Crap home to eat themselves and share with their loved ones.

What is a superfood? Superfoods far exceed functional food and—according to expert Diane Allen, a health writer, holistic clinical nutritionist and author of the book *Chia Seed*—they "are nutrient-dense and packed with antioxidants and other powerful health-promoting substances. As a rule, one needs to eat only a small amount of a superfood to get a big benefit."[1]

CHIA: OMEGA-3, ANTIOXIDANTS, CALCIUM AND HIGH-SOLUBLE FIBRE

With more omega-3 essential fatty acids than any other natural source, and loaded with antioxidants, protein, calcium and many other minerals, chia seeds seem almost too good to be true. And yet another of my favourite benefits is their soluble fibre, very gentle and healing for the digestive tract: chia seeds work to detoxify the gut, all the while keeping you feeling satisfied.[2]

Chia seeds provide stamina and endurance. And because they absorb so much water and are high in soluble fibre, they help release natural carbohydrate energy slowly into the bloodstream, making them a perfect staple for anyone with blood-sugar challenges—from diabetics to those who simply want to eliminate food cravings.

In the ancient Mayan language, *chia* meant "strength." History says a single tablespoon of this legendary superfood could sustain an Aztec warrior for an entire day. And the Tarahumara, the greatest long-distance runners on the planet, also have a long record of using this slow-burning rocket fuel.

When I discovered chia seeds in those early days of developing this cereal, I was so excited by how remarkably healthy they are—and by how easy they are to store and eat on the run. Simply adding a 2:1 ratio of hot or cold water to chia seeds expands them by 10 times and transforms them within five minutes into a tasty, pudding-like, easy-to-swallow meal.

BUCKWHEAT: PLANT-BASED PROTEIN AND POWERHOUSE NUTRITION

Buckwheat is one of the best sources of high-quality, easily digestible proteins in the plant kingdom. This fruit seed, related to rhubarb and sorrel, has a rich nutty flavour and is an excellent meat substitute with a 74-per cent protein-absorption rate. Very high in carbohydrates (80 percent) and with twice the fibre than oatmeal, this nutritional dynamo is also loaded with minerals and vitamins including niacin, manganese, iron, copper and immune-boosting zinc.[3]

Despite its name, buckwheat is not related to wheat and is 100 per cent gluten-free.

HULLED HEMP SEEDS: THE PERFECT BALANCE OF OMEGA-3 AND OMEGA-6

Like chia, hemp seeds contain more omega-3 essential fatty acids than wild salmon and are the ideal balance of omega-3 and omega-6. Our standard diet today provides heightened levels of omega-6, which can produce an inflammatory response in the body. Hulled hemp seeds fight bad cholesterol and take a strong role in regulating inflammatory responses. You will reap even more beautiful benefits from these essential fats—a healthier nervous system and improved skin and hair.[4] Hemp has been an invaluable source of food and fibre for the past 10,000 years.

100-PER CENT PLANT-BASED

Holy Crap, Skinny B and Holy Crap Plus Gluten Free Oats are the perfect start or finish to a daily plant-based diet.

A plant-based menu—whether based on a vegan diet or plant-focused eating plan of any variation—is increasingly being recommended for optimal well-being.

The World Health Organization recently acknowledged that encouraging people "to increase their consumption of nutritious plant-based foods could reduce heart disease and some cancers," in addition to reducing the methane emissions that are associated with animal-sourced foods and that are contributing to global warming.[5]

"I live in a dorm and am not always able to eat the healthiest foods. Your product has saved my digestive tract." —KARA

ALL ORGANIC INGREDIENTS

All the ingredients in our cereals are certified organic and our chia, buckwheat and hulled hemp seeds are raw, not baked, to ensure optimal life force and digestibility.

CERTIFIED GLUTEN FREE, GUARANTEED

While most cereals are produced and packed in a mega-facility with other products that may contain gluten, Holy Crap cereals are only made in our very own dedicated factory in Gibsons on the Sunshine Coast. Our facility has been certified gluten free, organic, kosher and nut free.

Holy Crap, Skinny B and Holy Crap Plus Gluten Free Oats will work for most people with food allergies and sensitivities, being organic, Non-GMO Project Verified, vegan, kosher, certified gluten-free and nut-free—and packaged in our very own HACCP-certified* facility to ensure these standards are never compromised. (*Hazard Analysis Critical Control Point is a globally recognized preventative food-safety management system.)

"I'm so glad I discovered this awesome cereal. My nine-year-old son, who has celiac disease, now has a favourite snack before bed. It helps him with his chronic constipation, plus he loves it." —CRYSTAL

INDIVIDUALLY PACKED TO PRECISE STANDARDS

While it might sound old-fashioned nowadays, we remain committed to hand mixing. Why? This ensures quality, because our people are checking every bag every day and adding the organic fruit with care to ensure it is in perfect condition. Each and every ingredient is measured to precise specifications with every bag reliably providing a consistent level of exceptional nutrition. Holy Crap cereals are served with confidence in health-care facilities around the world and recommended by many doctors and nurses, as well as the cancer-care organization InspireHealth.

It's the love that our staff puts into every pack that people feel.

NO SALT OR CHEMICAL ADDITIVES

Holy Crap cereals have never contained any chemical additives or preservatives; however, back in the early days, I would add a pinch of salt to every bag as homage to all the cooks in the world. But when a customer at the Granville Island Market asked, in the interest of making the cereal even healthier, if I could leave the salt out, I listened.

We became the only product in the cereal aisle that had no salt, along with no chemical additives. No one missed it, and people were happy and appreciative to have a natural choice without the usual negatives.

Holy Crap—Breakfast, Lunch or Dinner with Benefits

There are many paybacks to enjoying Holy Crap cereals as part of your daily eating:

INCREASED ENDURANCE AND ENERGY

Eaten with confidence by endurance athletes, space explorers, pregnant women, students, pilots, soldiers, business executives and people everywhere, Holy Crap increases endurance and energy, reduces food cravings and is the ideal food for running any marathon—whether that be getting through a busy day of work or running across the Sahara Desert.

> "This cereal keeps me full much longer than anything else I've tried and it's all natural and healthy. I have a sensitivity to gluten so this is perfect for me."—DEBBIE

Starting October 28, 2012, health warrior Deyl Kearin ran a 250-kilometre (155-mile) race across the Sahara, carrying all his own gear and supplies, to raise money for Run4Poverty. He fuelled up each morning with Skinny B cereal and coconut milk before trekking over the hottest desert on Earth.

STABILIZED BLOOD SUGAR

In Holy Crap, Holy Crap Plus Gluten Free Oats and Skinny B cereals a large portion of the carbohydrate content comes from fibre. These complex carbohydrates break down slowly in the body and maintain a steady stream of energy to the bloodstream. Simply speaking, the carbohydrates in our cereals are of the highest possible quality and will not cause the insulin or

sugar rushes you would receive from refined cereals. (And choose Skinny B if you are highly concerned about your blood sugar, as it does not contain the dried fruits found in Holy Crap or the maple syrup flakes added to Holy Crap Plus Gluten Free Oats.)

Try folding a few tablespoons of Holy Crap or Skinny B into pancake batter and your other favourite recipes to make them more filling and nutritious.

IMPROVED REGULARITY

I can tell you again about our high-soluble fibre and how our cereals help to keep you regular . . . but I think that in this case our name pretty much speaks for itself!

OPTIMIZED DIGESTION

Unlike flaxseeds, chia seeds do not need to be ground up. Chia seeds, along with buckwheat and hulled hemp seeds, are dynamos when it comes to preventing digestive distress. When soaked in milk, juice or water first, they optimize the digestive tract without absorbing valuable fluids from the body.

Holy Crap, 60 Recipes

While we started off suggesting Holy Crap for breakfast, enthusiastic customers have encouraged us to find more ways to work Holy Crap's health benefits into their day. This idea has led to a lot of delicious recipe development by my co-author Claudia Howard and me, and we now have 60 suggestions for ways you can enjoy eating our cereals for breakfast, yes, but also for lunch, dinner and dessert. Each recipe is super-simple and quick to prepare with just a very few easily found ingredients.

If you are short on time or just want to simplify your life—while at the same time taking good care of yourself and your family—this is the cookbook for you. Our simple ideas for home cooking will create delicious memories for your loved ones while nourishing them with some of the best plant-based food on the planet.

Every recipe contains one of our superfood cereals—Holy Crap, Skinny B or Holy Crap Plus Gluten Free Oats—which are available in stores from Canada to Kenya to Germany to Japan.

Many of the dishes in this collection are completely plant-based—and we note this fact wherever it applies. We begin with Breakfast Basics—from Slow Cooker Power Breakfast to Pumpkin Pie Overnight Oats—then move on to Silky Smoothies that pack a wallop of fibre and nutrition, and Perfect Parfaits and Power Packs—a big favourite with the kids!

Salads and Starters range from Quinoa Zucchini Clusters to Roasted Squash and Walnut , Savouries and Sides from Soba Rainbow Bowl with Green Chutney to Sweet Potato Kugel, and our grand finale of Naughty But Nice (Sweets) offers several luscious temptations, including Holy Crap Dark Chocolate Bark, truffles, cheesecake and peach crumble.

Give these recipes a try, adapting them to your taste or adding our cereals to your own favourite meals.

From all of our team, enjoy!

—Corin Mullins

RECIPES

A Few Notes about Ingredients

Growing up in Spain and France before moving to Canada as a girl, I was taught that home cooking from fresh ingredients was best—in fact, back then it was the *only* way to eat. We shopped in our own neighbourhood for local fruits and vegetables, and every bit of it was organic.

To this day, cooking reminds me that the simple rituals in life are often the most enjoyable. I like the act of chopping, for example, with its soothing rhythm. While I seem to have acquired just about all the slice-and-dice gadgets available on the planet, I'm realizing I don't use them much. Give me a knife and a board and some vegetables to cut up and I start to relax and sink into what I'm doing in the kitchen. And I like the act of cooking, right from scratch but keeping it simple too, the way my mother did.

When I choose food, I look for the freshest and healthiest produce I can find and, for me, that means choosing locally grown and organic—found in my community at a farmers' market or through a farm co-op. Along with buying locally grown organic fruits and vegetables, it's nice to lean to free-range eggs and poultry and locally caught wild seafood.

I'm a strong believer, too, in looking for fair trade certified options. I know from working directly with farmers to buy the ingredients that go into our cereals that when we choose fair trade bananas, cocoa, coconut, coffee, chocolate, olive oil and sugar, we are choosing to be the difference we want to see. And ensuring these choices are organic protects our world along with the workers who feed us.

About the Symbols

These symbols help identify recipes suitable for your dietary preferences. All the recipes in this book are appropriate for a gluten-free diet, but if you are sensitive to gluten, be sure to read the labels of packaged ingredients, such as miso paste, to make sure the brand you use is appropriate for your needs.

 These recipes contain milk-based ingredients.

These recipes contain no animal products and are suitable for vegans.

Gel Power

Skinny B gel is quick to make with a neutral taste. Add it to seed butters and hummus, or use it as a binder in pancakes, muffins, savoury loaves and stuffings. Use it instead of flour to thicken soups and sauces. Add minced garlic, herbs and a pinch of salt and pepper to Skinny B gel and pour it over vegetables as a flavoursome dressing. Blend the gel with tomatoes, herbs and spices for a speedy pasta sauce. To make, place 1 Tbsp (14 g) Skinny B cereal and 1 cup (250 mL) water in a jar. Shake well and let sit at least 10 minutes to thicken. It will keep in the fridge for up to 10 days.

Are you getting your daily essential Omega-3s?

Our bodies don't produce essential fatty acids like omega-3 and omega-6; therefore, we need to get them from our daily diet. Essential fatty acids decrease inflammation, support the nervous system and improve skin and hair.

Dietitians of Canada recommend the following daily amount of omega-3 for adults:

MEN	WOMEN	PREGNANT WOMEN	NURSING WOMEN
1.6g	1.1g	1.4g	1.3 g

Plant-based food sources of omegas, like chia and hulled hemp seeds, have less impact on the planet's resources. Fish oil, a common source of omega-3 in supplements, is subject to mercury and other industrial pollutants. Organizations like consumerlabs. com have even found some brands of fish oil contain rancid fatty acids that can harm your health, making plant-based sources of omega-3 better for you *and* the planet.

BREAKFAST BASICS

〰〰〰〰〰

Start your day on the right track with these gluten-free breakfast recipes. Our plant-based cereals are good for you and for the planet, as they're a natural source of protein, fibre, omega-3 and omega-6 fatty acids. From quick oats for weekdays when you're dashing out the door to pancakes for weekends when you have more time to savour a leisurely brunch, these recipes are so tasty you'll forget they're made with the healthiest cereal you'll ever eat.

〰〰〰〰〰

SLOW COOKER POWER BREAKFAST

MAKES 8 SERVINGS

1 cup (250 mL) gluten-free
  steel cut oats
½ cup (120 mL/90 g) Holy Crap
  cereal
5 cups (1.2 L) cold water
¼ cup (60 mL) plain non-fat
  Greek yogurt (optional)
Chopped fresh fruit, for
  garnish

On cold mornings, a bowl of hot cereal can be just the thing to start the day. If you have a slow cooker, set it to work overnight and you'll wake up to a nutritious hot breakfast. This recipe saves so much time that it's my go-to breakfast throughout the winter months. For variety, toast the oats before you slow cook them. Melt a little coconut oil (or unsalted butter) in a heavy frying pan, add the oats and stir for about five minutes until they darken slightly and smell like popcorn.

1. Place the steel cut oats and Holy Crap cereal in a slow cooker and stir in the water. Cover with the lid and cook on low for 10 hours.

2. To serve, divide into individual bowls, mix in a dollop of yogurt (optional) and garnish with fruit.

NUTRITION FACTS: PER 182 G SERVING. Calories (150) Total Fat (4.5 g) including Omega-3 (2 g) and Omega-6 (1.5 g) Total Carbohydrates (24 g) Dietary Fibre (4 g) Protein (9 g)
Provides 14% of your daily calcium needs based on a 2000-calorie diet.

APPLE PIE OVERNIGHT OATS

MAKES 2 SERVINGS

¼ cup (60 mL) gluten-free
 rolled oats or gluten-free
 steel cut oats

⅓ cup (80 mL) unsweetened
 almond milk

⅓ cup (80 mL) coconut milk

¼ cup (60 mL) unsweetened
 applesauce

1 Tbsp (15 mL) maple syrup or
 honey (optional)

1 Tbsp (15 mL/14 g) Holy Crap
 cereal

Sliced apples, for garnish

Here's a new twist on an old favourite. I've combined applesauce, uncooked oats and Holy Crap cereal for this gluten-free breakfast treat. The heavenly aroma alone will bring everyone running. Combining nutrition-packed Holy Crap cereal with wholesome oats gives an added boost to your morning meal. Like Holy Crap, oats are high in fibre and protein to keep you feeling energized and full for longer.

1. Place all of the ingredients except the sliced apples in a bowl or a glass container. Stir until well combined, then cover and refrigerate overnight.
2. In the morning, stir again and divide into two serving bowls. Garnish with sliced apples.

NUTRITION FACTS: PER 113 G SERVING. Calories (170) Total Fat (9 g) including Omega-3 (625 mg) and Omega-6 (500 mg) Total Carbohydrates (20 g) Dietary Fibre (2 g) Protein (4 g)

HOLY CRAP WITH APPLESAUCE

MAKES 1 SERVING

In a hurry? If you're tempted to skip breakfast because you're in a rush, try this plant-based breakfast recipe featuring Holy Crap cereal with applesauce. It's quick to prepare—and easy to take with you in a sealed container—so you can still incorporate a healthy breakfast into your busy morning. If you're watching your sugar intake or following an alkaline diet, an unsweetened strawberry or plum compote makes a great alternative to applesauce.

¼–½ cup (60–120 mL) unsweetened applesauce
2 Tbsp (30 mL/28 g) Holy Crap cereal
Spoonful of coconut cream (optional)

1. Place the applesauce in a bowl, stir in the Holy Crap cereal and let sit for 5 minutes. Stir again and garnish with coconut cream.

NUTRITION FACTS: PER 140 G SERVING. Calories (170)   Total Fat (6 g) including Omega-3 (2.5 g) and Omega-6 (1.5 g)   Total Carbohydrates (25 g) Dietary Fibre (8 g) Protein (6 g)
Provides 56% of your daily iron and 30% of your daily vitamin C needs based on a 2000-calorie diet.

HOLY CRAP WITH ALMOND MILK

MAKES 1 SERVING

2 Tbsp (30 mL/28 g) Holy Crap
  cereal
½ cup (120 mL) almond milk

You won't go wrong enjoying a bowl of almond milk and Holy Crap cereal. It's a quick, tasty and healthy way to start your day. Eat it plain, or add nuts or raisins for crunch or sweetness.

1. Pour the almond milk into a bowl, stir in the Holy Crap cereal and let sit for 5 minutes. Stir again and garnish as desired.

A high-fibre diet contributes to reducing cholesterol, stabilizing blood sugar and aiding in weight loss.

NUTRITION FACTS: PER 148 G SERVING. Calories (140) Total Fat (8 g) including Omega-3 (2.5 g) and Omega-6 (1.5 g) Total Carbohydrates (13 g) Dietary Fibre (67 g) Protein (7 g)
Provides 58% of your daily iron needs based on a 2000-calorie diet.

Why You Need to Soak Holy Crap and Skinny B

Unlike your average breakfast cereal where you just pour flakes into a bowl, add milk and dig in, Holy Crap and Skinny B are raw seed-based power foods that are optimized by soaking prior to eating. In fact, soaking is essential in many recipes: if you skip this step, your recipe will not turn out as expected, as both cereals will absorb moisture from other recipe ingredients. Or eaten as cereal without being soaked first, Holy Crap and Skinny B will be dry to swallow and less digestible.

Pre-soaking for at least five minutes will allow the seeds, especially the chia, to expand ten times. You'll literally see the cereal swell before your eyes, and the resulting gel-like consistency makes the nutrients much more bioavailable.

Soaking is also the delicious secret that made Jim Treliving of CBC's *Dragons' Den* quip, "Holy Crap . . . is this ever good!" as he emptied his own bowl and then reached over for Robert Herjavec's too. For each serving, I had mixed 2 tablespoons (30 mL/28 g) of Holy Crap cereal with about ¼ cup (60 mL) of vanilla hemp milk earlier that day. But as Brian and I had to wait most of the day before stepping into the *Dragons' Den*, the milk was being absorbed by the cereal—so every couple of hours I stirred in more. By the time we appeared on the set, the cereal was thick, smooth and creamy. You can achieve similar results by soaking the cereal overnight in the fridge and adding more liquid in the morning.

To save time when cooking with Holy Crap and Skinny B, pour the whole bag of cereal into 3 cups (750 mL) of water up to a week ahead of time and use ½ cup (125 mL) of expanded cereal in any recipe that calls for 2 Tbsp (30 mL/28 g) to be pre-soaked.

STEEL CUT OATS WITH HOLY CRAP, FOUR WAYS
MAKES 1 SERVING

1 cup (250 mL) water
¼ cup (60 mL) gluten-free steel cut oats
1 Tbsp (15 mL/14 g) Holy Crap cereal
½ cup (120 mL) plain non-fat Greek yogurt (optional)
½ cup (120 mL) chopped fresh fruit (optional)

This is four recipes in one! Steel cut oats are named for the steel blades that chop whole oat groats into pieces. Although they take a little longer to prepare than regular rolled oats, steel cut oats are chewier, nuttier and higher in soluble fibre (which is great and gentle for your gut). For a basic dairy-free breakfast, power up your steel cut oats by adding Holy Crap cereal. Then add yogurt (for protein and a creamy texture), fresh fruit (for a good dose of vitamins and antioxidants) or both yogurt and fresh fruit (for maximum nutrition and even more flavour). Any of these combinations will keep you energized all morning long. Two of our favourite topping combinations are fresh-picked blueberries and sliced bananas or tangy raspberries and apricots.

1. Bring the water to a boil in a medium saucepan. Stir in the oats, reduce the heat to low and simmer uncovered, stirring occasionally, for 10 to 15 minutes.
2. Stir in the Holy Crap cereal and cook for 5 minutes more.
3. Stir in yogurt or top with fresh fruit, or stir in yogurt *and* top with fresh fruit, if desired.

Tip: Cooked oatmeal will keep refrigerated in an airtight container for several days. Eat it cold or add a bit of water and heat gently in a pot on the stove before eating. It freezes well in individual portions, too.

NUTRITION FACTS: PER 132 G SERVING. Calories (150) Total Fat (5 g) including Omega-3 (1.25 g) and Omega-6 (1 g) Total Carbohydrates (20 g) Dietary Fibre (4 g) Protein (6 g)

PUMPKIN PIE OVERNIGHT OATS
MAKES 2 SERVINGS

Save time in the morning by making up this unforgettable breakfast treat the night before and letting it soak overnight. It's also perfect for Thanksgiving, even if you've already used up all the pumpkin purée for the pie. Just substitute two spoonfuls of pumpkin pie instead. Or consider serving these oats as a gluten-free Thanksgiving dessert in place of pumpkin pie.

¼ cup (60 mL/35 g) Holy Crap Plus Gluten Free Oats
½ cup (120 mL) unsweetened almond milk
¼ cup (60 mL) coconut milk
¼ cup (60 mL) pumpkin purée (or 2 Tbsp/30 mL leftover pumpkin pie, including the crust if it's gluten free)
1 Tbsp (15 mL) honey or maple syrup (optional)
1 Tbsp (15 mL) chopped pecans (optional, for garnish)

1. Place all of the ingredients except the chopped pecans in a bowl or a glass container. Stir until well combined, then cover and refrigerate overnight.
2. In the morning, stir again and divide into two serving bowls. Garnish with chopped pecans.

Why You Should Soak Oats Overnight

By soaking your organic oats in liquid overnight, they become easier to digest and the nutrients become more bioavailable, says our nutritionist Erika Weissenborn. It's true. An overnight soak—in any type of milk, yogurt, water or lemon water—breaks down both starches and the anti-nutrient phytic acid that inhibits mineral absorption, while increasing "resistant starch," a nutritional good guy that optimizes metabolism. Raw soaked oats are sweet, cake-like and delicious—and the perfect grab-and-go breakfast for a healthy start to the day.

NUTRITION FACTS: PER 140 G SERVING. Calories (190) Total Fat (10 g) including Omega-3 (625 mg) and Omega-6 (500 mg) Total Carbohydrates (21 g) Dietary Fibre (4 g) Protein (4 g)
Provides 77% of your daily vitamin A needs based on a 2000-calorie diet.

ULTIMATE BREAKFAST GRANOLA

MAKES TWENTY ⅓-CUP (80-ML) SERVINGS

1¼ cups (300 mL) gluten-free steel cut oats

1¾ cups (415 mL) gluten-free rolled oats

1 cup (250 mL/185 g) Holy Crap or Skinny B cereal

1⅓ cups (315 mL) whole raw almonds

¾ cup (180 mL) raw sunflower seeds

¾ cup (180 mL) shredded unsweetened coconut

1¼ cups (300 mL) chopped pecans

1¼ cups (300 mL) peanuts with skins

1 cup (250 mL) walnut pieces

½ cup (120 mL) whole raw sesame seeds

⅓ cup (80 mL) whole raw pumpkin seeds

½ cup (120 mL) agave nectar

½ cup (120 mL) maple syrup

4 tsp (20 mL) vanilla extract

½ cup (120 mL) coconut oil, melted

A special thanks to Kathy Smart, chef and nutritionist and the host of *Live the Smart Way*, North America's first gluten-free TV cooking show, for contributing this tasty breakfast granola recipe. I like to mix up a batch and portion it into individual servings, which I store in resealable plastic bags or small airtight containers. It's great served with nut milk or yogurt for breakfast, sprinkled on smoothies or salads, or eaten dry out of hand as a snack. I also use it as a quick topping for cooked sliced apples or applesauce. It's so versatile you'll find yourself doubling the batch.

1. Preheat the oven to 250F (120C). Line a baking sheet with parchment paper.
2. In a large bowl, mix all the dry ingredients together until well combined.
3. In a separate bowl, whisk together the agave nectar, maple syrup and vanilla extract.
4. Pour the melted coconut oil over the dry ingredients and mix well. Add the liquid mixture and stir until well mixed.
5. Spread the granola evenly over the baking sheet and bake, stirring every 15 minutes, until golden brown and very fragrant, about 1 hour.
6. Remove the granola from the oven and allow to cool on the baking sheet. Store in an airtight container at room temperature for up to 2 weeks.

NUTRITION FACTS: PER 172 G SERVING (⅓ CUP). Calories (390) Total Fat (26 g) including Omega-3 (1 g) and Omega-6 (1 g) Total Carbohydrates (25 g) Dietary Fibre (6 g) Protein (9 g)

OAT AND COTTAGE CHEESE PANCAKES

MAKES 1 SERVING (4 PANCAKES)

½ cup (120 mL/70 g) Holy Crap
 Plus Gluten Free Oats

½ medium banana, cut into
 chunks

½ tsp (2.5 mL) vanilla extract

1 tsp (5 mL) gluten-free
 baking powder

1 egg

¼ cup (60 mL) fat-free cottage
 cheese

2 Tbsp (30 mL) unsweetened
 almond milk

Olive oil, for coating the pan

Maple syrup, for topping

Raspberries, for garnish

Mint leaves, for garnish

Enjoy these golden pancakes for breakfast or brunch, or even for dinner. Leftover pancakes are also good as a snack at any time.

1. Place all ingredients, except the topping and garnishes, in a blender and process until completely smooth, about 30 seconds.
2. Lightly coat a large non-stick skillet or griddle with oil and heat over medium-low.
3. Spoon a quarter of the batter into the skillet and gently spread it out a bit with the back of the spoon. Cook until bubbles appear on top, 1 to 2 minutes. Gently flip the pancake and cook until the underside is golden, 1 to 2 minutes. Transfer to a plate.
4. Using a damp cloth, wipe the skillet clean. Add a bit more oil and repeat with the remaining batter.
5. Serve in a stack, topped with maple syrup and garnished with raspberries and mint leaves.

Very high in fibre and rich in both protein and calcium, a serving of these pancakes also covers your daily omega-3 requirement. The fibre fills you up, the omega-3 increases your concentration and the protein maintains your energy.

NUTRITION FACTS: PER 260 G SERVING. Calories (430) Total Fat (12 g) including Omega-3 (2 g) and Omega-6 (2 g) Total Carbohydrates (64 g) Dietary Fibre (9 g) Protein (20 g)
Provides 35% of your daily calcium and 34% of your daily iron needs based on a 2000-calorie diet.

OAT AND BANANA PANCAKES
MAKES 2 SERVINGS (3 LARGE PANCAKES OR 5–6 SMALL ONES)

2 medium bananas, cut into chunks (reserve a few chunks for garnish)

¾ cup (180 mL) unsweetened almond milk

1 tsp (5 mL) vanilla extract

1 cup (250 mL/140 g) Holy Crap Plus Gluten Free Oats

1½ tsp (7.5 mL) gluten-free baking powder

¼ tsp (1 mL) salt

Olive oil, for coating the pan

Plain yogurt or cultured coconut milk, for topping (optional)

Blueberries or other fresh fruit, for topping (optional)

Kids love pancakes—and so do Brian and I. The best part about pancakes is choosing the toppings. Go simple and healthy with fruit or peanut butter, or more decadent with maple syrup or chocolate chips. Our favourite is yogurt or cultured coconut milk with blueberries and bananas. Cultured milks are a non-dairy substitute for yogurt; they're full of fibre and made with live active cultures that support the digestive system.

1. Place the bananas, almond milk and vanilla in a blender and purée for 30 seconds until smooth. Add the oats, baking powder and salt and blend until the batter is well combined, about 1 minute. Set aside for a few minutes to thicken up.

2. The batter will be thicker than regular pancakes but still easily ladled into the pan. If it appears too thick, add a tablespoon or two of almond milk and blend again.

3. Lightly coat a large non-stick skillet or griddle with oil and heat over medium-low.

4. Using a ladle, drop ⅓ cup (80 mL) batter for large pancakes or ¼ cup (60 mL) for smaller ones into the skillet and gently spread out a bit with the back of the ladle. Cook until bubbles appear on top, 1 to 2 minutes. Gently flip the pancake and cook until the underside is golden, 1 to 2 minutes. Transfer to a plate.

5. Using a damp cloth, wipe the skillet clean. Add a bit more oil and repeat with the remaining batter.

6. Serve topped with yogurt, blueberries and sliced bananas (or your favourite toppings).

These pancakes are high in beta-glucan fibre to rev up your immune system.

NUTRITION FACTS: PER 155 G SERVING. Calories (140) Total Fat (2.5 g) including Omega-3 (0.5 g) and Omega-6 (0.5 g) Total Carbohydrates (30 g) Dietary Fibre (4 g) Protein (3 g)
Provides 40% of your daily iron and 22% of your daily calcium needs based on a 2000-calorie diet.

SKINNY B JAM

MAKES 8 SERVINGS (2 TBSP/30 ML EACH)

1 cup (250 mL) fresh or frozen berries (thawed)

1 Tbsp (15 mL/14 g) Skinny B (grind first if you prefer a smoother texture)

1 tsp (5 mL) freshly squeezed lemon or lime juice

The gelling effect of the chia seeds in Skinny B makes it a perfect alternative to using sugar and pectin in jam. And no cooking required! Skinny B's neutral flavour lets the fruit shine. I don't usually use any sweetener in this jam, as I've noticed the less processed sugar I eat, the sweeter fruit tastes, but you might want to add a little of your preferred sweetener if your fruit is especially tart. During the summer months Skinny B Jam is a great way to enjoy the abundance of local raspberries, strawberries and blackberries. In winter, this recipe works just as well with frozen fruit (that's been thawed). A squeeze of lime or lemon brightens the flavour. I've been known to add a teaspoon of finely minced jalapeño pepper, basil or mint when the ingredients and mood present themselves. Brian and I spread Skinny B Jam lavishly on pancakes and sometimes I add a teaspoon on top of Two-Ingredient cookies (page 73) before baking.

1. In a small bowl (a 2-cup glass measuring cup works perfectly), mash berries with a fork, stir in the Skinny B cereal and let sit for 5 minutes. Keeps refrigerated in a covered container for up to 3 days. Skinny B Jam freezes well, too.

 Tip: Frozen blueberries or cherries work even better than fresh, because freezing and thawing breaks down the skin of the fruit.

NUTRITION FACTS: PER 30 ML SERVING (2 TBSP). Calories (15) Total Fat (1 g) including Omega-3 (0.5 g) and Omega-6 (0.25 g) Total Carbohydrates (1 g) Dietary Fibre (0.5 g) Protein (0.5 g)

OATMEAL BANANA BAKE
MAKES 7 SERVINGS

Olive oil, for coating the
  ramekins
1 cup (250 mL) milk (nut or
  non-dairy)
1 cup (250 mL) organic apple
  juice
1 bag (530 mL/320 g) Holy
  Crap Plus Gluten Free Oats
1 or 2 bananas, sliced
Brown sugar to taste

Holy Crap Plus Gluten Free Oats mixed with apple juice
and nut milk—and then broiled to perfection—is one of my
favourite breakfasts. It makes a hearty treat that warms me
from the inside out.

1. Turn on the broiler. Lightly oil seven ¾ cup (180 mL)
   ramekins.
2. Place the milk and apple juice in a bowl, stir in the
   oats and let sit for 5 minutes. Stir again and spoon
   into the ramekins.
3. Top with sliced bananas, sprinkle with brown sugar
   and broil for about 5 minutes. Watch closely so that
   the sugar doesn't burn!
4. Remove from the oven and serve warm.

NUTRITION FACTS: PER 230 G SERVING. Calories (370)   Total Fat (9 g) including Omega-3 (0.5 g) and
Omega-6 (0.5 g)   Total Carbohydrates (68 g)   Dietary Fibre (10 g)   Protein (11 g)
Provides 38% of your daily iron and 22% of your daily calcium needs based on a 2000-calorie diet.

SILKY SMOOTHIES

~~~~~~~~~~~~~~~~~~~~~

Smoothies pack a wallop. They're full of vitamins, minerals, protein and fibre, and they're a perfect way to get additional servings of fruit and vegetables into your busy day. That's a lot of goodness in one delicious and satisfying drink. To save time, chop your fruit and vegetables ahead of time, portion them into individual servings and refrigerate (or freeze) them until needed. What an awesome way to get your daily nutrients in a hurry!

~~~~~~~~~~~~~~~~~~~~~

SMOOTH MOVE SMOOTHIE

MAKES 2 SERVINGS

¼ cup (60 mL) water

2 Tbsp (30 mL/28 g) Skinny B cereal

¾ cup (180 mL) plain non-fat Greek yogurt

¾ cup (180 mL) unsweetened almond milk

¼ cup (60 mL) sliced strawberries + a few more for garnish

½ medium banana + ½ for garnish

This is a crowd pleaser. Kids love the fruity taste of the strawberries and bananas. Adults love that it has 4 grams of fibre, almost twice the mimimum recommended for breakfast by Dietitians of Canada—and that's why we've called this drink our Smooth Move smoothie.

1. Pour the water into a bowl, stir in the Skinny B cereal and let sit for 5 minutes.

2. Place all the ingredients, except the garnishes, in a blender and process until smooth. Pour into glasses, garnish with sliced strawberries and bananas, and serve.

The chia in Skinny B cereal makes it an ideal addition to any smoothie to create the perfect thick consistency.

NUTRITION FACTS: PER 275 G SERVING. Calories (200) Total Fat (6 g) including Omega-3 (1.5 g) and Omega-6 (1 g) Total Carbohydrates (29 g) Dietary Fibre (4 g) Protein (8 g)
Provides 24% of your daily calcium needs based on a 2000-calorie diet.

BANANA OAT SMOOTHIE

MAKES 2 SERVINGS

½ cup (120 mL/70 g) Holy Crap
  Plus Gluten Free Oats
1½ cups (350 mL) water
1 medium banana, frozen
1½ cups (350 mL) unsweetened
  almond milk
1 cup (250 mL) ice cubes
Fresh fruit, for garnish

Brian and I drink smoothies all the time, and we love this one because it's rich and thick like a milkshake. We call it the Snowstorm, which is our version of a Dairy Queen Blizzard®! Keep a supply of peeled bananas in the freezer to add a cold creaminess to all your smoothies.

1. Place the Holy Crap Plus Gluten Free Oats in a medium bowl, add the water and stir well. Let sit for 5 minutes.
2. Place all the ingredients, except the fruit garnish, in a blender and process until smooth. Pour into glasses, garnish with fresh fruit and serve.

NUTRITION FACTS: PER 465 G SERVING. Calories (290) Total Fat (11 g) including Omega-3 (3 g) and Omega-6 (2 g) Total Carbohydrates (40 g) Dietary Fibre (9 g) Protein (11 g)
Provides 92% of your daily iron needs based on a 2000-calorie diet.

REFRESHING RHUBARB SMOOTHIE

MAKES 2 SERVINGS

This simple smoothie is perfect for spring, when your garden (or the local farmers' market) is overflowing with rhubarb and strawberries. Claudia Howard, our vice-president of marketing, loves the tang of rhubarb and chooses not to sweeten her purée at all, but you can add a natural sweetener if you prefer. If you have extra purée, use it in place of applesauce in our Holy Crap with Applesauce (page 24) breakfast recipe.

RHUBARB PURÉE

2 stalks rhubarb, cut into
  1-in (2.5-cm) pieces
¼ cup (60 mL) water
Honey or maple syrup (optional)

1. Place the rhubarb and water in a medium saucepan and heat on medium until bubbling. Reduce the heat to low and cook until soft, 10 to 12 minutes.
2. Remove from the heat, stir in the honey or maple syrup if using and let cool completely. Leftovers will keep refrigerated in an airtight container for 3 to 4 days.

RHUBARB SMOOTHIE

¼ cup (60 mL) water
2 Tbsp (30 mL/28 g) Skinny B cereal
¾ cup (180 mL) plain non-fat
  Greek yogurt
¾ cup (180 mL) unsweetened
  almond milk
½ cup (120 mL) sliced
  strawberries
½ cup (120 mL) rhubarb purée
  (see above)

1. Pour the water into a bowl, stir in the Skinny B cereal and let sit for 5 minutes.
2. Place all the ingredients in a blender and process until smooth. Pour into glasses and serve.

The cooked rhubarb in this colourful smoothie contains many powerful antioxidants (including lycopene). Calcium and vitamin K also contribute to a healthy digestive tract.

NUTRITION FACTS: PER 300 G SERVING. Calories (150) Total Fat (5 g) including Omega-3 (1.5 g) and Omega-6 (1 g) Total Carbohydrates (16 g) Dietary Fibre (3 g) Protein (9 g)
Provides 24% of your daily calcium needs based on a 2000-calorie diet.

BERRYLICIOUS SMOOTHIE
MAKES 2 SERVINGS

½ cup (120 mL) water

2 Tbsp (30 mL/28 g) Skinny B
   cereal

½ cup (120 mL) fresh or frozen
   unsweetened strawberries

½ cup (120 mL) fresh or frozen
   unsweetened raspberries

1 cup (250 mL) plain non-fat
   Greek yogurt

1 cup (250 mL) unsweetened
   almond milk

Fresh berries, for garnish

Mint leaves, for garnish

One of the best things about living on the West Coast is berry season. Every year, I look forward to filling buckets with local berries and freezing them for the winter months. I like strawberries and raspberries in combination, but you could use just one berry or substitute any of your other favourites—blueberries, blackberries, huckleberries, Saskatoon berries… try them all! (If you're using fresh berries, throw in a few ice cubes to increase the thickness.) This smoothie comes together in just a few minutes, so it's perfect when you need breakfast in a hurry or a midafternoon pick-me-up.

1. Pour the water into a bowl, stir in the Skinny B cereal and let sit for 5 minutes.
2. Place all the ingredients, except the garnishes, in a blender and process until smooth. Pour into glasses, garnish with fresh berries and mint and serve.

NUTRITION FACTS: PER 420 G SERVING. Calories (180)   Total Fat (5.5 g) including Omega-3 (1.5 g) and Omega-6 (1.25 g)   Total Carbohydrates (26 g)   Dietary Fibre (7 g)   Protein (11 g)
Provides 50% of your daily vitamin C and 38% of your daily calcium needs based on a 2000-calorie diet.

AZTEC AVOCADO SMOOTHIE
MAKES 2 SERVINGS

¼ cup (60 mL) water

2 Tbsp (30 mL/28 g) Skinny B cereal

½ cup (120 mL) cultured coconut milk (or cultured almond milk)

½ cup (120 mL) unsweetened almond milk (or other non-dairy milk)

½ avocado

½ medium banana

Celery leaves or other vegetable leaves, for garnish

Long before I started making Skinny B and Holy Crap cereals, the Aztecs (and the Mayans) were cultivating and eating chia seeds, which were ground into flour, pressed for their oil or mixed with water. The seeds were prized as medicine because they gave messengers enough strength to run all day. This is my ode to them. Creamy and tropical, it's a powerhouse of micronutrients, fibre and complex sugars, and it's also high in heart-healthy fats.

1. Pour the water into a bowl, stir in the Skinny B cereal and let sit for 5 minutes.
2. Place all the ingredients, except the garnish, in a blender and process until smooth. Pour into glasses, garnish as desired and serve. Ta-da! You're done and on your way.

Cultured milks are a non-dairy alternative to yogurt; they're a good source of fibre and made with live active cultures that support the digestive system.

NUTRITION FACTS: PER 200 G SERVING. Calories (220) Total Fat (13 g) including Omega-3 (1.5 g) and Omega-6 (1 g) Total Carbohydrates (23 g) Dietary Fibre (8 g) Protein (6 g)
Provides 15% of your daily calcium needs based on a 2000-calorie diet.

BLUEBERRY SWIRL SMOOTHIE

MAKES 2 SERVINGS

1 cup (250 mL) water, divided in half

2 Tbsp (30 mL/28 g) Skinny B cereal

1 cup (250 mL) fresh or frozen unsweetened blueberries

½ cup (120 mL) plain non-fat Greek yogurt

½ cup (120 mL) unsweetened almond milk

½ medium banana, frozen

In August and September, the Sunshine Coast is loaded with various berries just waiting to be picked for smoothies (and pies and jams and jellies and crumbles and eating out of hand…). If you're not lucky enough to have blueberries growing in your backyard, seek them out at your local farmers' market or substitute whatever berry is in season in your neighbourhood. It takes only an extra minute to turn this blueberry smoothie into a visual feast.

1. Pour ½ cup (120 mL) water into a bowl, stir in the Skinny B cereal and let sit for 5 minutes.
2. Place the blueberries and the remaining ½ cup (120 mL) water in a blender and process until smooth. Pour into a small bowl.
3. Rinse the blender, then add the yogurt, milk, banana and soaked cereal and process until smooth. Divide between 2 tall glasses.
4. Using a spoon, drop some of the blueberry purée down the inside of each glass and swirl it through the smoothie. Serve.

Smoothies to Go

When you whip up your smoothie, go ahead and make an extra glass to go. Smoothies are the ultimate in fast food and while they're best fresh, they will still contain fibre, antioxidants and phytonutrients even after 12 hours in the refrigerator. Just be sure to seal your pick-me-up tightly in a glass jar filled to the top to reduce oxidation. And for good measure, squeeze in a healthy dash of lemon to add vitamins and help keep it fresh.

Blueberries are packed with phytonutrients and fibre, making them a great way to start your day.

NUTRITION FACTS: PER 356 G SERVING. Calories (170) Total Fat (5 g) including Omega-3 (1.5 g) and Omega-6 (1 g) Total Carbohydrates (26 g) Dietary Fibre (6 g) Protein (7 g)
Provides 19% of your daily calcium needs based on a 2000-calorie diet.

MANGO CARROT SMOOTHIE

MAKES 2 SERVINGS

1 cup (250 mL) water

¼ cup (60 mL/45 g) Skinny B cereal

3 cups (710 mL) frozen mango chunks

2 cups (475 mL) fresh carrot juice

Mango chunks, for garnish

Slices of carrot, for garnish

Naturally sweet and delicious, this smoothie is a great year-round option, but it's particularly good on dark and dreary days when the bright-orange colour provides a welcome lift.

1. Pour the water into a bowl, stir in the Skinny B cereal and let sit for 5 minutes.
2. Place all the ingredients, except the garnishes, in a blender and process until smooth. Pour into glasses, garnish with mango and carrot and serve.

This icy-cold treat is high in fibre and very high in vitamin C. The carrots and mangoes also make it an excellent source of beta-carotene, which helps to build a strong immune system and healthy skin.

NUTRITION FACTS: PER 300 G SERVING. Calories (170)   Total Fat (7 g) including Omega-3 (3 g) and Omega-6 (2 g)   Total Carbohydrates (30 g)   Dietary Fibre (5 g)   Protein (5 g)
Provides 45% of your vitamin C needs based on a 2000-calorie diet.

KALE CUCUMBER SMOOTHIE
MAKES 2 SERVINGS

½ cup (120 mL) water
¼ cup (60 mL/45 g) Skinny B cereal
½ medium cucumber, unpeeled and roughly chopped
6 large kale leaves or 2 cups (475 mL) baby kale leaves
1 cup (250 mL) pineapple chunks
Handful of ice cubes (optional)
Lemon wedges, for garnish
Baby kale leaves, for garnish

Is kale on your weekly shopping list? It's one of the healthiest vegetables on the planet, with a high concentration of the antioxidant vitamins A, C and K. Kale is rich in minerals and very detoxifying. Paired with pineapple, cucumber and Skinny B, this smoothie is refreshing at any time, but it's especially cooling on a hot summer's day—and doubly so if you add a handful of ice cubes to the blender when you process the smoothie.

1. Pour the water into a bowl, stir in the Skinny B cereal and let sit for 5 minutes.
2. Place all the ingredients, except the garnishes, in a blender and process until smooth. Pour into glasses, garnish with a lemon wedge and a baby kale leaf, and serve.

NUTRITION FACTS: PER 228 G SERVING. Calories (120)   Total Fat (8 g) including Omega-3 (3 g) and Omega-6 (2 g)   Total Carbohydrates (19 g)   Dietary Fibre (4 g)   Protein (5 g)
Provides 87% of your daily vitamin C and 55% of your daily vitamin A needs based on a 2000-calorie diet.

GINGER CARROT SMOOTHIE

MAKES 2 SERVINGS

½ cup (120 mL) water

¼ cup (60 mL/45 g) Skinny B cereal

1 medium banana, frozen

1 cup (250 mL) fresh carrot juice

1 cup (250 mL) plain non-fat Greek yogurt

1-in (2.5-cm) peeled fresh ginger root, chopped

½ cup (120 mL) ice cubes

Wedges of blood orange, for garnish

Here the spicy zing of ginger pairs perfectly with the sweetness of the carrots—proof that what's good for us also tastes great, as ginger is an anti-inflammatory and soothes digestion. Try adding other fresh herbs and spices, such as mint or parsley, to your smoothies to increase their flavour and their nutritional value.

1. Pour the water into a bowl, stir in the Skinny B cereal and let sit for 5 minutes.
2. Place all the ingredients, except the blood orange, in a blender and process until smooth. Pour into glasses, garnish with a wedge of blood orange and serve.

Both ginger and carrots are powerful immune system boosters.

NUTRITION FACTS: PER 350 G SERVING. Calories (290)   Total Fat (7.5 g) including Omega-3 (3 g) and Omega-6 (2.5 g)   Total Carbohydrates (42 g)   Dietary Fibre (7 g)   Protein (14 g)
Provides 20% of your daily calcium needs based on a 2000-calorie diet.

SPINACH SMOOTHIE

MAKES 2 SERVINGS

¼ cup (60 mL) water

2 Tbsp (30 mL/28 g) Skinny B
  cereal

½ cup (120 mL) cultured
  coconut milk

½ cup (120 mL) unsweetened
  almond milk

½ cup (120 mL) packed, washed
  baby spinach leaves

½ medium banana

Handful of ice cubes

Herb leaves and edible flowers,
  for garnish (optional)

Holy Crap is a favourite among athletes as well. Sunshine Coast local, Kyla Richey of Robert's Creek, BC, is on the Canadian National Volleyball Team and calls our cereals her secret weapon, giving her the fuel she needs for her intense training. She explains, "It's easy to add that necessary protein boost to start my day off in the right way."

1. Pour the water into a bowl, stir in the Skinny B cereal and let sit for 5 minutes.
2. Place all the ingredients, except the garnishes, in a blender and process until smooth. Pour into a glass, garnish with herbs and edible flowers, and serve.

NUTRITION FACTS: PER 217 G SERVING. Calories (170) Total Fat (7 g) including Omega-3 (1.5 g) and Omega-6 (1 g) Total Carbohydrates (25 g) Dietary Fibre (7 g) Protein (6 g)
Provides 46% of your daily vitamin A needs based on a 2000-calorie diet.

MARVELLOUS MATCHA SMOOTHIE

MAKES 2 SERVINGS

½ cup (120 mL) water

¼ cup (60 mL/45 g) Skinny B cereal

1 cup (250 mL) frozen vanilla yogurt

1 cup (250 mL) unsweetened almond milk

2 tsp (10 mL) green matcha powder

Leo Tabibzadegan is one of our customers and he writes, "I've always been a fan of Skinny B cereal and all its nutritional benefits. One day I decided to combine the goodness of Skinny B with my addiction to matcha green tea, and this smoothie was the delicious result. Every cell in my body jumped for joy and happiness and the world became a better place. Now, combining all of my favourite things in one drink has become my daily routine for breakfast or for a snack on the go."

Matcha is a shade-grown green tea in which the stems and veins are removed and the rest of the leaf is ground to a powder. The leaves contain caffeine and antioxidants, yet are less harsh than coffee. Leo says, "Matcha was used in ancient spiritual ceremonies to help clear the mind and invoke a Zen-like state. When you combine that with all the benefits packed into Skinny B cereal, you've got your mind and body covered." Try this smoothie in the morning or at any time of day you need a little extra zip.

1. Pour the water into a bowl, stir in the Skinny B cereal and let sit for 5 minutes.
2. Place all the ingredients in a blender and process until smooth. Pour into glasses and serve.

NUTRITION FACTS: PER 238 G SERVING. Calories (270) Total Fat (9 g) including Omega-3 (3 g) and Omega-6 (2 g) Total Carbohydrates (33 g) Dietary Fibre (11 g) Protein (17 g)
Provides 30% of your daily calcium needs based on a 2000-calorie diet.

ICED COFFEE SMOOTHIE

MAKES 2 SERVINGS

½ cup (120 mL) water
2 Tbsp (30mL/28 g) Skinny B cereal
1½ cups (350 mL) brewed coffee
1 cup (250 mL) chocolate almond milk
Small scoop of vanilla non-dairy frozen dessert
Handful of ice cubes

When the weather turns warm and you want your coffee, cereal and frozen dessert all at the same time, this delicious mocha-flavoured smoothie is the answer. For a caffeine-free version, try roasted chicory root instead of coffee. This plant has a familiar coffee taste, yet it's full of antioxidants, regulates blood sugar levels and boosts digestion. This smoothie is the perfect healthy non-dairy drink for breakfast on the run or an afternoon pick-me-up.

1. You guessed it... Pour the water into a bowl, stir in the Skinny B cereal and let sit for 5 minutes.
2. Place all the ingredients in a blender and process until smooth. Pour into a glass and serve.

NUTRITION FACTS: PER 350 G SERVING. Calories (200) Total Fat (12 g) including Omega-3 (1.5 g) and Omega-6 (1 g) Total Carbohydrates (16 g) Dietary Fibre (4 g) Protein (6 g)
Provides 15% of your daily calcium needs based on a 2000-calorie diet.

PERFECT PARFAITS
& POWER PACKS

Whether you prefer your energy to go in a glass or in your hand, these recipes will tide you over to your next meal. Breakfast parfaits make small, balanced meals of protein, carbohydrates and fat that appeal to even the pickiest eaters because the layers of cereal, fruit and yogurt look beautiful, taste great and are easy to assemble. Vary the fruit (fresh or thawed from frozen) and opt for plain Greek yogurt (or dairy-free cultured coconut or almond milk) over flavoured yogurt that is high in sugar.

O CANADA BREAKFAST PARFAIT

MAKES 1 SERVING

½ cup (120 mL) plain non-fat Greek yogurt, divided in half
2 Tbsp (30 mL/28 g) Holy Crap cereal
½ cup (120 mL) chopped strawberries
Mint leaves, for garnish

Canada Day holds a special significance for me. My family immigrated to Calgary from Europe when I was six, and I remember my dad studying for his citizenship test and how proud we all were when we became Canadian citizens. These days, I still make a point of celebrating Canada Day… with our Canadian-made cereals. Dorothy Raymond, our executive assistant, served this parfait during a Canada Day event in Central Park, New York City. Don't let the good looks deceive you! This tasty breakfast parfait is packed with protein and fibre to keep you going strong all morning.

1. In a glass, layer half of the yogurt, followed by Holy Crap cereal, the remaining yogurt and the strawberries. Garnish with mint leaves.
2. To eat, stir to mix the cereal with the yogurt and wait a few minutes for the cereal to soften.

NUTRITION FACTS: PER 227 G SERVING. Calories (240)   Total Fat (8 g) including Omega-3 (2.5 g) and Omega-6 (2 g)   Total Carbohydrates (27 g)   Dietary Fibre (6 g)   Protein (14 g)
Provides 76% of your daily vitamin C and 30% of your daily calcium needs based on a 2000-calorie diet.

ALL-AMERICAN BREAKFAST PARFAIT

MAKES 1 SERVING

½ cup (120 mL) plain non-fat Greek yogurt, divided in thirds

2 Tbsp (30 mL/28 g) Holy Crap cereal

¼ cup (60 mL) sliced strawberries

¼ cup (60 mL) blueberries

Mint leaves, for garnish

Celebrate the red, white and blue! Chef Guy Mitchell, formerly at the White House in Washington, DC, now travels across the US with the White House Chef Tour. He performs food demonstrations at culinary schools, fundraisers, and wine and food festivals. He often prepares dishes using Holy Crap products and created this recipe just for us. Try this parfait on the Fourth of July—or any other day of the year.

1. In a glass, layer a third of the yogurt, followed by Holy Crap cereal, another third of the yogurt, the strawberries, the remaining yogurt and, finally, the blueberries. Garnish with mint leaves.

2. To eat, stir to mix the cereal with the yogurt and wait a few minutes for the cereal to soften.

NUTRITION FACTS: PER 310 G SERVING. Calories (260) Total Fat (6 g) including Omega-3 (2.5 g) and Omega-6 (2 g) Total Carbohydrates (38 g) Dietary Fibre (7 g) Protein (14 g)
Provides 54% of your daily vitamin C and 29% of your daily calcium needs based on a 2000-calorie diet.

RHUBARB PARFAIT

MAKES 1 SERVING

Rhubarb is a special plant. It's a vegetable, though we usually treat it like a fruit. And it's one of the few vegetables that is a not available in supermarkets year round. Which makes seeing its stalks poke through the soil in spring, and pinken as the weather warms, all the more exciting. Here we've paired this superfood with Holy Crap for a tangy breakfast treat. Rhubarb is low in carbohydrates and high in vitamin C, fibre and potassium. Look for rhubarb in early spring at your local farmers' market.

RHUBARB PURÉE

2 stalks rhubarb, cut into 1-in (2.5-cm) pieces
¼ cup (60 mL) water
Honey or maple syrup (optional)

1. Place the rhubarb and water in a medium saucepan and heat on medium until bubbling. Reduce the heat to low and cook until soft, 10 to 12 minutes.
2. Remove from the heat, stir in the honey or maple syrup to taste, if using, and let cool completely. The purée will keep refrigerated in an airtight container for 3 to 4 days.

 RHUBARB PARFAIT

½ cup (120 mL) lemon or plain non-fat Greek yogurt
2 Tbsp (30 mL/28 g) Holy Crap cereal
½ cup (120 mL) rhubarb purée (see above) (reserve 1 Tbsp/15 mL for garnish)
Edible flowers, for garnish

1. In a glass, layer half of the yogurt, followed by Holy Crap cereal, the rhubarb purée and the remaining yogurt. Garnish with the reserved rhubarb purée and edible flowers.
2. To eat, stir to mix the cereal with the yogurt and wait a few minutes for the cereal to soften.

NUTRITION FACTS: PER 300 G SERVING. Calories (250) Total Fat (6 g) including Omega-3 (2.5 g) and Omega-6 (2 g) Total Carbohydrates (36 g) Dietary Fibre (6 g) Protein (11 g)
Provides 27% of your daily calcium needs based on a 2000-calorie diet.

BLACKBERRY BREAKFAST PARFAIT
MAKES 1 SERVING

¼ cup (60 mL) water
2 Tbsp (30 mL/28 g) Holy Crap
  cereal
½ cup (120 mL) plain non-fat
  Greek yogurt (reserve a
  spoonful for garnish)
½ cup (120 mL) fresh
  or thawed blackberries
  (reserve 1 for garnish)
Wedge of fresh lemon
Honey, for drizzling

Kathy Smart, TV show host, best-selling author, chef, keynote speaker and nutritionist, contributed this recipe. "This gluten-free breakfast not only tastes amazing, it stabilizes your blood sugar," she says. And that means you'll stay full of energy, control your weight, stabilize your mood, sharpen your memory and balance your hormones." That's a pretty good return on one breakfast parfait!

1. Pour the water into a bowl, stir in the Holy Crap cereal and let sit for 5 minutes.
2. In a glass, layer the yogurt, followed by the soaked Holy Crap cereal and the blackberries. Garnish with a dollop of yogurt and top with a blackberry.
3. Add a squeeze of lemon and a drizzle of honey for the perfect touch of sweetness.

NUTRITION FACTS: PER 255 G SERVING. Calories (260) Total Fat (8 g) including Omega-3 (2.5 g) and Omega-6 (2 g) Total Carbohydrates (27 g) Dietary Fibre (10 g) Protein (19 g)
Provides 40% of your daily vitamin C and 22% of your calcium needs based on a 2000-calorie diet.

BASICALLY BEAUTIFUL BREAKFAST PARFAIT

MAKES 1 SERVING

¼ cup (60 mL) water
2 Tbsp (30 mL/28 g) Holy Crap cereal
½ cup (120 mL) plain non-fat Greek yogurt
½ cup (120 mL) chopped mixed fruit
Mint leaves, for garnish

A gorgeous breakfast parfait entices even the fussiest eater, and this one does double duty by providing the perfect ratio of omega-3 and omega-6 fatty acids to fuel your brain and help you concentrate throughout the day. Enjoy the simplicity and versatility of this three-ingredient recipe (cereal, yogurt, fruit), which is very low in cholesterol, low in sodium, high in calcium, high in dietary fibre and very high in vitamin C.

1. Pour the water into a bowl, stir in the Holy Crap cereal and let sit for 5 minutes.
2. In a glass, layer the soaked Holy Crap cereal, followed by the yogurt and the fruit. Garnish with one or more mint leaves.

NUTRITION FACTS: PER 255 G SERVING. Calories (250)   Total Fat (6 g) including Omega-3 (2.5 g) and Omega-6 (2 g)   Total Carbohydrates (34 g)   Dietary Fibre (6 g)   Protein (13 g)
Provides 56% of your daily vitamin C and 30% of your daily calcium needs based on a 2000-calorie diet.

SANTA'S PARFAIT
MAKES 1 SERVING

¾ cup (180 mL) plain non-fat
Greek yogurt, divided into
fifths (reserve 1 Tbsp/15 mL
for garnish)
2 Tbsp (30 mL/28 g) Holy Crap
cereal
¼ cup (60 mL) chopped
raspberries or strawberries
(reserve 1 for garnish)
¼ cup (60 mL) chopped kiwis or
green grapes

Don't skip out on your health during the holidays! This
high-fibre snack will stabilize your blood sugar and make
you feel full for hours, so you'll be less tempted to overeat.
Since strawberries and raspberries are not in season at
this time of year, use frozen. Alternatively, use cranberries
steeped in orange juice for the red berries.

1. In a glass, layer one-fifth of the yogurt, followed by
    Holy Crap cereal, a second layer of yogurt and half
    the raspberries (or strawberries). Top with a third
    layer of yogurt, half the kiwis (or grapes), a fourth
    layer of yogurt and the remaining raspberries (or
    strawberries). Finish with the rest of the yogurt and
    the kiwis (or grapes).
2. Garnish with a final dollop of yogurt and a raspberry
    (or strawberry).
3. To eat, stir to mix the cereal with the yogurt and wait
    a few minutes for the cereal to soften.

Tip: Make the garnish look like a cute little Santa's
hat by adding a teeny-tiny dab of yogurt on top of the
final raspberry (or strawberry).

NUTRITION FACTS: PER 320 G SERVING. Calories (320) Total Fat (9 g) including Omega-3 (2.5 g) and
Omega-6 (2 g) Total Carbohydrates (40 g) Dietary Fibre (8 g) Protein (18 g)
Provides 133% of your daily vitamin C and 43% of your daily calcium needs based on a 2000-calorie diet.

HOLY CRAP ENERGY BALLS
MAKES 8 ENERGY BALLS

5 oz (140 g) Medjool dates,
  pitted (about 9 dates)
¼ cup (60 mL) raw almonds
1 Tbsp (15 mL) raw unsalted
  sunflower seeds
2 Tbsp (30 mL/28 g) Holy Crap
  cereal
2 Tbsp (30 mL) dried
  cranberries
1½ tsp (7.5 mL) raw unsalted
  pumpkin seeds
½ tsp (2.5 mL) cinnamon
Pinch of salt

I love dates, and I use them in both sweet and savoury dishes. Early in my career as a flight attendant, dates were my "fast food"—quick snacks that fit in my carry-on and didn't need refrigeration. These energy balls made with dates are fun and easy for kids to make, and they're a great alternative to packaged granola bars, which are usually packed with hidden oils and sugars. Dates are quite high in fruit sugar, so these are a treat, but they are also a good source of fibre and they have 50 per cent more potassium by weight than bananas. All that potassium is good for your heart and your digestion.

1. In a food processor, pulse the dates and almonds until they are mostly ground up. Some larger pieces are okay.
2. Transfer the date mixture to a medium bowl, add the remaining ingredients and mix well.
3. Pinch off a tablespoon-sized amount of dough and roll it between your palms to form a ball (or flatten it like a cookie if you prefer). Repeat with the remaining dough. Arrange the energy balls on a plate and refrigerate until needed. They will keep refrigerated in an airtight container for several days.

These energy balls are a good high-energy snack for on the go. They won't cause an extreme spike in blood sugar and will leave you with more sustained energy.

NUTRITION FACTS: PER 42 G SERVING (1 ENERGY BALL). Calories (180) Total Fat (9 g) including Omega-3 (312 mg) and Omega-6 (250 mg) Total Carbohydrates (22 g) Dietary Fibre (4 g) Protein (5 g)

FRUIT 'N' NUT BARS

MAKES 16 BARS

½ cup (120 mL) water, divided in half

2 Tbsp (30 mL/28 g) Holy Crap cereal

2 eggs (or egg substitutes)

½ cup (120 mL) nut butter

¼ cup (60 mL) maple syrup

¼ cup (60 mL) brown sugar (optional)

½ tsp (2.5 mL) salt

1 cup (250 mL) gluten-free flour

1½ cups (350 mL) gluten-free rolled oats

3 Tbsp (45 mL) chopped walnuts (or pecans)

⅓ cup (80 mL) Medjool dates, pitted and chopped

3 Tbsp (45 mL) raisins

3 Tbsp (45 mL) dried cranberries

Who doesn't like fruit and nuts together? Especially good is any fruit you've picked and dried yourself, either in the oven or in a food dehydrator. Make this recipe as is for breakfast or an afternoon snack, or experiment with your own combinations. Thank you to Lisa Cantkier, founder of GlutenFreeFind.com, for contributing this recipe.

1. Preheat the oven to 350F (175C). Line an 8-in (20-cm) square baking dish with parchment paper.

2. Pour ¼ cup (60 mL) water into a bowl, stir in the Holy Crap cereal and let sit for 5 minutes. Set aside.

3. In a large bowl, beat the eggs and then add the soaked cereal. Add the nut butter, maple syrup, brown sugar (if using), salt and the remaining ¼ cup (60 mL) water and stir until well combined.

4. Stir in the flour, oats, nuts, dates, raisins and cranberries and mix well. Spread the batter evenly into the baking dish and bake for 15 to 17 minutes, until the edges become golden. Allow to cool completely before cutting into squares. The bars will keep refrigerated in an airtight container for up to 1 week.

NUTRITION FACTS: PER 60 G SERVING (1 BAR). Calories (210) Total Fat (8 g) including Omega-3 (150 mg) and Omega-6 (125 mg) Total Carbohydrates (23 g) Dietary Fibre (5 g) Protein (7 g)
Provides 16% of your daily iron needs based on a 2000-calorie diet.

NUT BUTTER COOKIES

MAKES 12 COOKIES

1 cup (250 mL/140 g) Holy Crap Plus Gluten Free Oats

½ cup (120 mL) nut butter (soy butter, almond butter, peanut butter)

¼ cup (60 mL) water

¼ cup (60 mL) vegan semi-sweet chocolate chips

Leave the oven off! These ridiculously easy no-bake cookies made with a handful of ingredients take only a few minutes to make. The rich taste comes from that perfect pairing of nut butter and semi-sweet chocolate chips. Since they need to refrigerate for a couple of hours before you can eat them, make them ahead of time so they're ready when you need them.

1. In a large bowl, mix together all of the ingredients until well combined. If your mixture is too thick or dry, add a little more water.
2. Scoop a tablespoon of dough into the palm of your hand, roll it into a ball, flatten it and put it on a plate lined with parchment paper. Repeat with the remaining dough.
3. Refrigerate the plate of cookies, uncovered, for 2 hours. Yes, it's that easy! The cookies will keep refrigerated in an airtight container for several days, if they last that long!

NUTRITION FACTS: PER 40 G SERVING (1 COOKIE). Calories (150) Total Fat (8 g) including Omega-3 (208 mg) and Omega-6 (167 mg) Total Carbohydrates (17 g) Dietary Fibre (3 g) Protein (5 g) *Provides 13% of your daily iron needs based on a 2000-calorie diet.*

Why Oats Are Awesome (and Not Just for Breakfast)

Packed with fibre that is highly beneficial to the digestive system, oats are also among the most heart-healthy foods in the world. Cholesterol is a chemical substance produced in the body and consumed in foods of animal origin, and it comes in two types: low-density lipoprotein (LDL) and high-density lipoprotein (HDL). In excessive amounts, LDL cholesterol can latch onto artery walls, causing narrowing and making it difficult for blood to travel freely. When digested, oats become a gel in the stomach and intestines that captures LDL lipoprotein—bad cholesterol—*before* it reaches the bloodstream. Furthermore, oats contribute HDL lipoprotein—good cholesterol, which absorbs the excess LDL lipoprotein.

Oats also contain healthy doses of thiamin, magnesium, phosphorous, manganese, molybdenum and iron, among other vitamins and minerals. Low on the glycemic index, oats also help to maintain glucose levels and often prove to be beneficial to those with diabetes. While oats do not contain gluten, they are likely to come in contact with it in many packaging facilities, so people with sensitivities are strongly advised to choose only products from a certified gluten-free facility.

TWO-INGREDIENT GLUTEN FREE OAT COOKIES

MAKES 24 COOKIES

3 bananas
1 bag (11 oz/320 g) Holy Crap
   Plus Gluten Free Oats
Vegan chocolate for drizzling
   (optional)

There isn't an easier cookie recipe to make and bake than these two-ingredient breakfast cookies created by our office manager, Lori Pepper. Made with Holy Crap Plus Gluten Free Oats, they have a satisfying chewiness from the oats and a natural sweetness from the bananas and from the organic dried fruit and maple flakes in the cereal.

1. Preheat the oven to 350F (175C). Line a baking sheet with parchment paper.
2. Mash the bananas in a large bowl. Stir in the oats and let the batter sit for 5 minutes. Stir again.
3. Drop tablespoonfuls of the batter onto the baking sheet and bake for 11 to 13 minutes. Turn off the oven, open the oven door and allow the cookies to cool in the oven for 20 minutes. The cookies will keep refrigerated in an airtight container for several days. They freeze well, too.

Tip: For a special treat, melt some vegan dark chocolate in the top of a double boiler (or a stainless steel bowl inside a metal colander over a saucepan of water on low heat), allow to cool slightly, then use the tines of a fork to drizzle the melted chocolate over the cooled cookies.

NUTRITION FACTS: PER 85 G SERVING (3 COOKIES). Calories (190) Total Fat (4 g) including Omega-3 (1 g) and Omega-6 (1 g) Total Carbohydrates (36 g) Dietary Fibre (6 g) Protein (6 g)
Provides 18% of your daily iron needs based on a 2000-calorie diet.

CRANBERRY MUFFINS
MAKES 18 MUFFINS

This delicious recipe is adapted from Kathy Smart's gluten-free cookbook, *Live the Smart Way*. Thank you! These muffins are great for breakfast or as a snack when you're on the go, as they're high in protein to fill you up and stimulate your metabolism. And because they're made from whole foods, they're much more nutritious than store-bought muffins—even with the lemon glaze. Make an extra batch of these high-energy muffins and freeze them in resealable plastic bags so you always have some on hand. Serve them with a cup of tea or coffee.

2½ cups (600 mL) ground almonds (or almond flour)
½ tsp (2.5 mL) baking soda
½ tsp (2.5 mL) gluten-free baking powder
¼ tsp (1 mL) salt
1½ tsp (7.5 mL) cinnamon
½ cup (120 mL/90 g) Skinny B cereal
½ tsp (2.5 mL) vanilla extract
½ cup (120 mL) honey
3 eggs
1½ cups (350 mL) fresh or frozen cranberries + a few extra for garnish

1. Preheat the oven to 325F (160C). Line 18 medium muffin cups with paper liners.
2. In a bowl, combine the ground almonds (or almond flour), baking soda, baking powder, salt and cinnamon.
3. In a separate bowl, whisk together the Skinny B cereal, vanilla, honey and eggs until well combined and let sit for 5 minutes, then whisk again. Add the dry ingredients and mix well. Stir in the cranberries until evenly mixed.
4. Fill each cup ⅔ full and bake for 20 to 23 minutes. Cool on a baking rack, then remove the paper liners, drizzle with the lemon glaze and garnish with cranberries before serving. Leftovers can be refrigerated in an airtight container for several days.

LEMON GLAZE (OPTIONAL)

½ cup (120 mL) icing sugar
Juice from 1 lemon
Lemon zest

1. Place all the ingredients in a bowl. Whisk vigorously until smooth.

NUTRITION FACTS: PER 45 G SERVING (1 MUFFIN, WITH GLAZE). Calories (160) Total Fat (10 g) including Omega-3 (0.5 g) and Omega-6 (0.5 g) Total Carbohydrates (12 g) Dietary Fibre (4 g) Protein (6 g) *Provides 23% of your daily iron needs based on a 2000-calorie diet.*

Clean Eating—You Can't Fake *Real* Food

It's healthy to come clean when reviewing your menu, and clean eating—enjoying real food—is the way to go if you suffer from inflammation, illness or food sensitivities, or simply want to optimize your energy and health. Think an apple a day—or orange or banana—when it comes to snacks. There's no need to gravitate to processed or refined foods when nature has provided such perfect gifts. Always opt for fresh, organic, local and seasonal—embracing ethical food choices wherever you can, whether to you this means going vegan, choosing free-range eggs instead of caged, or picking pasture-raised meat instead of factory farmed.

Clean eating also means slowing down to savour your supper, and sharing it with family or friends if you can. Instead of eating on the run, be ready for those hunger pangs with something simple and satisfying in your purse or backpack. A Holy Crap or Skinny B cereal cup is one idea, but veggie sticks, yogurt, nuts or fruit are others. Eat more often but less at a time—nutritionist Erika Weissenborn suggests striving to be 80 per cent full—and when you are nourishing yourself as nature intended, you'll feel energized by every delicious bite.

SALADS & STARTERS

Lunches, picnics and cocktail parties often call for lighter fare. To make healthier food choices, I plan ahead by making and freezing batches of food when I have the time and by carrying my lunchtime salad in a jar so I'm not tempted to buy something on the run. The crackers and spread are incredibly versatile, too: take them as a snack on your next bike ride, camping weekend or family holiday. Or serve them on the deck with a bottle of wine.

VEGGIE SALAD IN A JAR

MAKES 2 SERVINGS

Nothing says summer more than crisp greens and fresh veggies. This is the recipe to make after harvesting produce from your garden or returning from the farmers' market. Enjoy this salad on its own for lunch, serve it as a side dish, at a picnic or top it with seafood (or cooked chickpeas or fava beans) for a heartier main course. Make this salad in a jar for easy transport or mix it up on a salad plate instead.

LEMON VINAIGRETTE

¼ cup (60 mL) extra-virgin olive oil

1 Tbsp (15 mL) freshly squeezed lemon juice

Salt and pepper to taste

1. In a small bowl, whisk together all the ingredients until well combined. Set aside.

VEGETABLE SALAD

¼ cup (60 mL) grape tomatoes, cut in half

¼ cup (60 mL) chopped yellow and orange bell peppers

2 Tbsp (30 mL/28 g) Holy Crap cereal

¼ cup (60 mL) chopped zucchini, cut in ¼-in slices and then quartered

2 cups (475 mL) mixed baby greens or baby spinach leaves

1. Divide the vinaigrette between two 16-oz (500 mL) glass jars with lids. Placing half the ingredients in each jar, top the vinaigrette with the tomatoes and bell peppers, followed by layers of cereal and zucchini. Finish with the baby greens or spinach. Seal the jars.
2. Shake well before eating.

NUTRITION FACTS: PER 180 G SERVING WITH 2 TBSP (30 ML) DRESSING. Calories (325) Total Fat (28 g) including Omega-3 (1.5 g) and Omega-6 (1 g) Total Carbohydrates (15 g) Dietary Fibre (4 g) Protein (6 g) *Provides 142% of your daily vitamin C and 62% of your daily vitamin A needs based on a 2000-calorie diet.*

FRUIT AND NUT SALAD IN A JAR
MAKES 2 SERVINGS

Did you know that adding nuts or seeds to vegetables and fruit increases our ability to absorb their phytonutrients? These naturally occurring compounds give fruit and vegetables their colour and protect the plants from disease. In our bodies, they provide anti-inflammatory and antioxidant properties. Make this salad in a jar in the morning and it will still be crisp when you're ready to eat it at lunchtime.

 CREAMY LEMON DRESSING

3 Tbsp (45 mL) olive oil
  mayonnaise or plain non-fat
  Greek yogurt
1 Tbsp (15 mL) freshly squeezed
  lemon juice
Salt and pepper to taste

1. In a small bowl, whisk together all the ingredients until well combined. Set aside.

FRUIT AND NUT SALAD

2 cups (475 mL) romaine lettuce
  (roughly ⅓ of a head), torn
  into bite-sized pieces, divided
  in half
1 stalk celery, sliced
½ apple (red or green), unpeeled
  but chopped and tossed in
  lemon juice
½ cup (120 mL) seedless red
  grapes, cut in half
¼ cup (60 mL) walnuts (optional)
1 Tbsp (15 mL/14 g) Skinny B cereal

1. Divide the dressing between two 16-oz (500-mL) glass jars with lids. Placing half the ingredients in each jar, top the dressing with half of the lettuce, followed by layers of celery, apple, grapes, walnuts and cereal. Finish with the remaining lettuce. Seal the jars.
2. Shake well before eating.

Satisfying and nutrient-dense salads like this one will keep you on track throughout the day. Making the right choices for lunch prevents the dreaded mid-afternoon energy crash.

NUTRITION FACTS: PER 160 G SERVING WITH 2 TBSP (30 ML) DRESSING. Calories (135) Total Fat (4.5 g) including Omega-3 (1 g) and Omega-6 (0.5 g) Total Carbohydrates (23 g) Dietary Fibre (6 g) Protein (5 g) *Provides 84% of your daily vitamin A needs based on a 2000-calorie diet.*

QUINOA ZUCCHINI CLUSTERS
MAKES 40 INDIVIDUAL CLUSTERS

I grew up cooking delicious multi-course meals with my mother. These days, although Brian and I still love to cook and often entertain visitors, we try to keep things a bit simpler and healthier. These clusters are always popular; they're easy to make and they feed a crowd. Best of all, three of these quinoa clusters contain fewer than 100 calories. Serve them as a savoury appetizer with a glass of wine, and then tuck any leftovers into your lunch bag for a snack the next day.

Olive oil for oiling muffin tins

¼ cup (60 mL) water

2 Tbsp (30 mL/28 g) Skinny B cereal

2 cups (475 mL) cooked quinoa (about ¾ cup/180 mL uncooked)

1 cup (250 mL) shredded zucchini

1 Tbsp (15 mL) chopped green onions, white part only

1 pkg (5.2 oz/150 g) Boursin cheese or other soft cheese

2 large eggs

Salt to taste

Parsley or chives, for garnish

1. Preheat the oven to 350F (175C). Lightly oil two 24-cup mini-muffin tins.
2. Pour the water into a bowl, stir in the Skinny B cereal and let sit for 5 minutes.
3. In a large bowl, combine the cooked quinoa, zucchini and green onions until well mixed. Add the cheese, using a spoon to break it up and work it into the other ingredients.
4. Using a whisk, mix the eggs into the soaked cereal until well combined. Pour into the quinoa mixture and stir until evenly combined. Season with salt to taste.
5. Drop 1 Tbsp (15 mL) of batter into each cup of a mini-muffin tin and bake for 12 to 14 minutes, or until the edges begin to brown.
6. Allow to cool in the tins for 5 minutes before unmolding. Serve warm, topped with chives or parsley. Leftovers will keep refrigerated in an airtight container for several days.

NUTRITION FACTS: PER 12 G SERVING (1 CLUSTER). Calories (30) Total Fat (3 g) including Omega-3 (75 mg) and Omega-6 (62 mg) Total Carbohydrates (3 g) Dietary Fibre (1 g) Protein (1 g)

APPLE CHEDDAR BITES

MAKES 40 INDIVIDUAL MINI MUFFINS

Cheddar and apple are a classic pairing, and these make-ahead appetizers are perfect for entertaining. I always keep a batch of these bites in the freezer to serve when last-minute guests drop by for a drink.

Olive oil for oiling muffin tins
¼ cup (60 mL) water
2 Tbsp (30 mL/28 g) Holy Crap cereal
2 cups (475 mL) cooked quinoa (about ¾ cup/180 mL uncooked)
1 cup (250 mL) grated green apple
⅔ cup (160 mL) grated sharp cheddar cheese
2 large eggs
Salt to taste
Sprigs of parsley, for garnish

1. Preheat the oven to 350F (175C). Lightly oil two 24-cup mini-muffin tins.
2. Pour the water into a bowl, stir in the Holy Crap cereal and let sit for 5 minutes.
3. In a large bowl, combine the cooked quinoa and grated green apple until well mixed. Add the cheese and stir gently until evenly incorporated.
4. Using a whisk, mix the eggs into the soaked cereal until well combined. Pour into the quinoa mixture and stir until evenly combined. Season with salt to taste.
5. Drop 1 Tbsp (15 mL) of batter into each cup of a mini-muffin tin and bake for 12 to 14 minutes, or until the edges begin to brown.
6. Allow to cool in the tins for 5 minutes before unmolding. Serve warm, topped with a sprig of parsley. Leftovers will keep refrigerated in an airtight container for several days.

Sweet and savoury, this recipe is a great protein and fibre-packed indulgence that's much more exciting than cheese and crackers.

NUTRITION FACTS: PER 13 G SERVING (1 MINI-MUFFIN). Calories (30)   Total Fat (2.5 g) including Omega-3 (62 mg) and Omega-6 (50 mg)   Total Carbohydrates (3 g)   Dietary Fibre (1 g)   Protein (1 g)

TWO-INGREDIENT SKINNY B CRACKERS
MAKES 12 CRACKERS

You won't find a simpler crispy cracker recipe. These Two-Ingredient Skinny B Crackers are gluten free, dairy free and vegan. They're wonderful on their own or served with either a sweet or savoury topping, such as the Roasted Squash and Walnut Spread (page 90), nut butters, sliced avocado and salsa. The riper the banana you use, the sweeter the crackers will be.

1 banana
½ cup (120 mL/90 g) Skinny B cereal

1. Preheat the oven to 350F (175C). Line a baking sheet with parchment paper.
2. In a large bowl, mash the banana with the back of a fork. Stir in the Skinny B cereal until well combined, then let the batter sit for 5 minutes. Stir again.
3. Drop tablespoonfuls of the batter onto the baking sheet. Flatten each mound with the back of the spoon and gently round the edges with your fingers. Bake for 20 to 25 minutes.
4. Remove from oven and slide the parchment paper with the crackers gently onto a cooling rack. The crackers will crisp up as they cool completely. Remove and discard the parchment paper. Serve on a platter. Store leftover crackers in an airtight container at room temperature for several days.

NUTRITION FACTS: PER 11 G SERVING (1 CRACKER). Calories (14)   Total Fat (1.5 g) including Omega-3 (1 g) and Omega-6 (0.5 g)   Total Carbohydrates (3 g)   Dietary Fibre (1 g)   Protein (1 g)

ARTISAN CRACKERS
MAKES ABOUT 80 CRACKERS

1 cup (250 mL/185 g) Skinny
  B cereal, ground in a coffee
  grinder
½ cup (120 mL) shredded
  Parmesan cheese
1½ tsp (7.5 mL) chopped fresh
  rosemary
2 large eggs
Sea salt, for sprinkling on
  crackers

Homemade crackers are even more crisp, delicious and healthy than store-bought. Be creative with the flavours: substitute different herbs or other hard cheeses. Serve these crackers, which are packed with protein and essential fats, on their own, or with cheese and a dollop of pepper jelly.

1. Preheat the oven to 350F (175C). Have ready 3 or 4 baking sheets and a roll of parchment paper.
2. In a large bowl, mix together all the ingredients, except the salt, and let sit for 5 minutes. The dough will be stiff.
3. Divide the dough into 3 or 4 pieces. Cut 2 pieces of parchment paper big enough to cover the baking sheet. Place a piece of dough on top of the first piece of parchment, cover it with the second piece of parchment and transfer to a cutting board. Using a rolling pin, roll the dough into a rectangle the size of your baking sheet. Remove the top layer of parchment, leaving the dough sitting on the bottom piece of parchment, and, with a sharp knife, score the dough into 1½- to 2-in (4- to 5-cm) squares.
4. Slide the parchment with the dough onto a baking sheet, sprinkle with sea salt and bake for 10 minutes (or a few minutes longer if you prefer a crispier cracker).
5. Remove the partially cooked dough from the oven, and wearing oven mitts, place a wooden cutting board on top of the baking sheet and invert both the baking sheet and the board together so the dough is transferred to the board.
6. Line the baking sheet with a new sheet of parchment. Peel off and discard the top piece of parchment, and slide the dough from the cutting board back onto the new sheet. Bake for another 3 minutes.

7. Allow to cool on the counter for 5 minutes, then break into individual crackers along score lines.
8. Repeat with the remaining dough. These crackers will keep in an airtight container at room temperature for 1 week.

NUTRITION FACTS: PER 6 G SERVING (1 CRACKER). Calories (20)   Total Fat (1 g) including Omega-3 (38 mg) and Omega-6 (32 mg)   Total Carbohydrates (1 g)   Dietary Fibre (1 g)   Protein (1 g)

SQUASH AND WALNUT SPREAD

MAKES 2 CUPS (475 ML)

2 lb (900 g) winter squash, such as butternut, cut into large pieces and seeds removed

3 Tbsp (45 mL) olive oil, divided in thirds

½ medium onion, finely chopped

Salt

2 Tbsp (30 mL) finely chopped fresh mint

Pinch (0.5 mL) freshly grated nutmeg

¼ cup (60 mL) finely chopped walnuts, lightly toasted

⅓ cup (80 mL) grated Parmesan cheese

2 Tbsp (30 mL/28 g) Skinny B cereal

Freshly ground black pepper

Whole walnuts, for garnish

Sprigs of parsley, for garnish

I find cooking a great way to relax, and I love to try new recipes. The bookshelves in our home are crammed with more than 200 cookbooks, though these days I often prop my iPad on the counter and cook from a recipe I've found online. This delicious spread, adapted from a *New York Times* recipe, is the perfect accompaniment to the Artisan Crackers (page 88) or Two-Ingredient Skinny B Crackers (page 86). It also makes a great dip for raw vegetables or a flavourful filling for sandwiches.

1. Heat the oven to 425F (220C). Line a baking sheet with aluminum foil and lightly oil the foil.
2. Arrange the squash in a single layer on the baking sheet and rub or toss with 1 Tbsp (15 mL) olive oil. Bake, turning with tongs every 15 minutes, until tender, 40 to 60 minutes. Remove from the oven and allow to cool.
3. Peel the squash and place the flesh in the bowl of a food processor fitted with the steel blade. Pulse several times, scrape down the sides of the bowl, then purée until smooth. Set aside, still in the food processor.
4. Heat 1 Tbsp (15 mL) olive oil in a large heavy skillet on medium heat. Add the onions and a generous pinch of salt and reduce the heat to medium-low. Cook, stirring often, until very tender, sweet and lightly caramelized, about 20 minutes. Remove from the heat and add to the squash.
5. To the food processor, add the mint, nutmeg, walnuts, Parmesan, Skinny B cereal and the remaining 1 Tbsp (15 mL) olive oil. Pulse until smooth and well combined. Season to taste with salt and pepper. Spoon into a serving dish and garnish with whole walnuts and sprigs of parsley. Leftovers will keep refrigerated in an airtight container for several days.

This rich and creamy spread is high in beta carotene and low in fat.

NUTRITION FACTS: PER 26 G SERVING (1 TBSP). Calories (30)   Total Fat (2.5 g) including Omega-3 (95 mg) and Omega-6 (75 mg)   Total Carbohydrates (1 g)   Dietary Fibre (1 g)   Protein (1 g)

FRUIT SALAD WITH HOLY CRAP OR SKINNY B

MAKES 1 SERVING

¾ cup (180 mL) chopped fresh
  fruit
1 Tbsp (15 mL) coconut cream
  (or plain non-fat Greek
  yogurt)
1 Tbsp (15 mL/14 g) Holy Crap
  or Skinny B cereal
Edible flowers, for garnish

Warm summer days mean an abundance of sweet, juicy fresh fruit, and what better way to celebrate them than by making fruit salad. Choose whatever fruit is in season— peaches, plums, apricots and cherries in midsummer; figs, pears and apples in the fall; or even citrus fruit in the colder months.

1. Arrange the fruit in a serving bowl. Top with a dollop of coconut cream (or yogurt) and sprinkle Holy Crap or Skinny B cereal on top. Garnish with edible flowers.

The added protein from the cereal and yogurt (or coconut cream) helps the body to digest the fruit more slowly, which maintains blood sugar levels for longer.

NUTRITION FACTS: PER 213 G SERVING. Calories (150) Total Fat (3.5 g) including Omega-3 (1.25 g) and Omega-6 (1 g) Total Carbohydrates (25 g) Dietary Fibre (4 g) Protein (6 g)
Provides 91% of your daily vitamin C and 46% of your daily vitamin A needs based on a 2000-calorie diet.

SAVOURIES & SIDES

~~~~~~~~~~

Although I'm guilty of eating cereal for dinner on occasion, most people don't think of including it in their savoury suppertime meals. Well, they're missing out! Here are several great examples of how adding nuts and seeds to popular dishes adds nutrition, crunch and flavour. Stir them into sauces and stir-fries, or just sprinkle them over your meal. What family favourite recipes can you reinvent with Skinny B or Holy Crap cereals?

~~~~~~~~~~

SOBA RAINBOW BOWL WITH GREEN CHUTNEY

MAKES 4 SERVINGS FOR A LIGHT LUNCH, OR 2 SERVINGS FOR A
HEARTY DINNER

4 oz (112 g) dry soba noodles
1 cup (250 mL) Green Chutney
  (page 97)
1 cup (250 mL) kale buds
  or broccoli florets, lightly
  steamed
1 small cooked yam, cut into
  cubes
⅓ cup (80 mL) shredded beet
⅓ cup (80 mL) shredded purple
  cabbage
½ avocado, sliced
2 hard-boiled eggs, peeled and
  halved (or firm tofu, cut into
  cubes and grilled or sautéed)
1 tsp (5 mL/5 g) Skinny B
  cereal

To ensure a balanced diet, health experts recommend
"eating the rainbow" when selecting produce. This one-bowl
meal is overflowing with colour, making it visually appealing
and loaded with vitamins. Try combining your favourite
seasonal produce, including green, orange, red and purple
toppings. Soba noodles made with 100 percent buckwheat
flour are naturally gluten free, but check the packaging, as
some brands do contain wheat flour.

1. Cook the soba according to the package directions
   or follow the traditional Japanese method: bring
   a large pot of water to a boil, add the noodles to
   the pot and separate by stirring. When the water
   comes to a boil again, add 1 cup (250 mL) cold water.
   Repeat 2 to 3 more times until the noodles are fully
   cooked but not mushy. Drain the soba in a colander
   and rinse with cool water. Let the noodles sit while
   you assemble the other ingredients.
2. Toss the cold soba noodles with ⅔ cup (160 mL)
   Green Chutney and divide between bowls.
3. Arrange a portion of the veggies, avocado and egg (or
   tofu) on top of each bowl. Garnish with a sprinkle of
   Skinny B cereal and a dollop of the remaining chutney.

NUTRITION FACTS: PER DINNER-SIZE SERVING (520 g). Calories (590) Total Fat (19 g) including Omega-3
(3 g) and Omega-6 (2 g) Total Carbohydrates (84 g) Dietary Fibre (11 g) Protein (23 g)
*Provides 96% of your daily vitamin C needs and 81% of your daily vitamin A needs based on
a 2000-calorie diet.*

GREEN CHUTNEY

MAKES 1¾ CUPS (415 ML)

¼ cup (60 mL/45 g) Skinny B cereal

1 clove garlic (or 2 cloves for garlic lovers)

1 small jalapeño pepper, ribs and seeds removed, or ½ tsp (2.5 mL) red chili flakes

½ tsp (2.5 mL) ground cumin

2 tightly packed cups (475 mL) fresh cilantro, including stems

1 tightly packed cup (250 mL) fresh mint leaves, stems removed

3 Tbsp (45 mL) water

½ cup (120 mL) fresh lime juice

½ cup (120 mL) raw unsalted cashews

½ tsp (2.5 mL) salt

Use this incredibly versatile take on traditional Indian green chutney not only in the Soba Rainbow Bowl but as an easy appetizer, served with pappadums or corn chips. It's also excellent with grilled meats, fish or tofu and high in vitamins A and C, as well as iron and calcium. Make sure to rinse the cilantro and mint well to remove grit, and then just shake off some of the excess water.

1. Place the Skinny B cereal in a food processor and pulse briefly to break down the seeds a bit. Add the garlic, jalapeño or chili, and cumin and process until well minced. Then add the cilantro, mint, water and lime juice and pulse until the greens are finely chopped but not puréed.

2. Add the raw cashews and process briefly, stopping while the nuts still have some texture.

3. Scrape the chutney into an airtight container and refrigerate for at least 1 hour to allow the flavours to blend. Make the chutney up to 2 days before you plan to serve it. It will keep refrigerated in an airtight container for 1 week.

NUTRITION FACTS: PER 30 ML SERVING (2 TBSP). Calories (90) Total Fat (5 g) Total Carbohydrates (7 g) Dietary Fibre (2 g) Protein (4 g)
Provides 42% of your daily vitamin A needs based on a 2000-calorie diet.

SKINNY B CRISPY CRAB CAKES

MAKES 10–12 CRAB CAKES

Dungeness crabs are a familiar sight in the waters of the Sunshine Coast, and their slightly sweet meat is delicious steamed, boiled or made into these crispy cakes. Serve these crab cakes individually as an appetizer or arrange two or three on a bed of mixed greens to make a delicious protein-packed meal. Thanks to Charlene SanJenko of PowHERhouse for inspiring and supporting women through her speaker series and events, and for creating this delicious recipe. The flavour of the olive oil comes through in this recipe, so choose one you like. Our favourite is the Sunshine Coast Olive Oil Company's "butter" flavour.

SPICY CREAM

⅓ cup (80 mL) plain non-fat Greek yogurt

2 Tbsp (30 mL) olive oil mayonnaise

1 tsp (5 mL) hot chili-garlic sauce (or more to taste)

1. In a small bowl, stir together the yogurt with the mayonnaise and chili-garlic sauce until well combined. Cover and refrigerate until needed.

CRAB CAKES

Olive oil in spritzer

⅔ cup (160 mL/125 g) Skinny B cereal

2 tsp (10 mL) olive oil

2 green onions, green and white parts, thinly sliced (reserve a few pieces for garnish)

1 medium green bell pepper, finely diced

1 jalapeño pepper, finely diced

1 Tbsp (15 mL) finely grated fresh ginger root

2 cloves garlic, minced

1 lb (454 g) claw crabmeat (or imitation crabmeat), picked over for cartilage

1 tsp (5 mL) finely grated lime zest (optional)

2–3 Tbsp (30–45 mL) fresh lime juice

¼ cup (60 mL) finely chopped fresh cilantro leaves

1 large egg, beaten

1 Tbsp (15 mL) olive oil mayonnaise

½ tsp (2.5 mL) salt

1 or 2 pkg (1.16 oz/33 g) Herb Simply Protein Chips (or rice crackers)

Dash or 2 of chipotle spice (optional)

Wedges of lime, for serving

1. Preheat the oven to 425F (220C). Spritz a baking sheet with olive oil.

2. Place the Skinny B cereal in a small heatproof bowl and just barely cover with boiling water. Let sit for 5 minutes. Set aside.

3. Heat the olive oil in a non-stick skillet over medium-high. Add the green onions, bell pepper and jalapeño and cook until the peppers are slightly soft, about 3 minutes. Stir in the ginger and garlic and cook for 1 minute more. Set aside to cool slightly.

4. In a food processor, chop the crabmeat. Place it in a large mixing bowl and add the onion-pepper mixture. Add the lime zest and juice, cilantro, egg, soaked cereal, mayonnaise and salt. Stir and knead very well until combined.

5. Rinse and dry the food processor and add the Simply Protein Chips (or rice crackers). Process until the chips have the texture of bread crumbs. (You will probably use 2 small bags.) Arrange the crumbs on a shallow plate, add a generous dash or two of chipotle spice and mix well.

6. Using your hands, pinch of about 1½ Tbsp (22 mL) of the crab mixture, form it into a crab cake and gently roll it in the crumbs. Set it on the baking sheet. Repeat with the remaining crab mixture.

7. Spritz the top of the crab cakes with olive oil to coat lightly. Bake the crab cakes until golden on the bottom, 12 to 15 minutes. Gently turn them over and cook for another 12 to 15 minutes.

8. Garnish the crab cakes with green onions and serve on a platter or individual plates with the spicy cream and wedges of lime. Lean eating never tasted so fine!

NUTRITION FACTS: PER 250 G SERVING (2 CRAB CAKES PLUS 2 TBSP/30 ML SAUCE). Calories (225) Total Fat (11 g) including Omega-3 (1.5 g) and Omega-6 (1 g) Total Carbohydrates (13 g) Dietary Fibre (2 g) Protein (16 g)

Provides 59% of your daily vitamin C and 31% of your daily calcium needs based on a 2000-calorie diet.

SKINNY B-ENCRUSTED SALMON
MAKES 6 SERVINGS

6 Tbsp (90 mL) plain non-fat
  Greek yogurt
3 Tbsp (45 mL) honey
1 cup (250 mL/185 g) Skinny
  B cereal
½ cup (120 mL) finely chopped
  pecans
Six 4-oz (112-g) salmon fillets,
  skin on
Salt and pepper to taste

Wild salmon is a traditional food on the West Coast, where it has sustained the First Nations for centuries. Here on the coast, we are fortunate to be able to buy our fish fresh from the boat, so we know exactly when it was caught, by whom and by what method. Make sure you buy only sustainably fished wild Pacific salmon; not only will it taste better, it will preserve our oceans and the fish for future generations. This recipe comes from Guy Mitchell, former chef at the White House in Washington, DC. Serve this salmon with mixed seasonal vegetables such as zucchini, yellow squash, broccoli, cauliflower and sliced carrots. Or try it with steamed baby spinach that's been seasoned with salt and pepper.

1. Preheat the oven to 400F (205C). Line a baking sheet with parchment paper.
2. In a bowl, whisk together the yogurt and honey. In a separate wide, shallow bowl, combine the Skinny B cereal and pecans.
3. Season each salmon fillet with salt and pepper and place it, skin side down, on the baking sheet. Spoon an equal amount of the yogurt mixture over each fillet, using the back of the spoon to spread it evenly and completely coat the flesh side of the fish. Spoon the Skinny B mixture over the yogurt coating, pressing it into the fish to create an even crust.
4. Measure the fillets at their thickest part and bake for 10 minutes per inch of thickness, or until the salmon just flakes when tested with a fork.
5. Divide the fillets among individual plates and serve immediately.

NUTRITION FACTS: PER 200 G SERVING (1 FILLET). Calories (530)   Total Fat (32 g) including Omega-3 (4 g) and Omega-6 (2.5 g)   Total Carbohydrates (26 g)   Dietary Fibre (11 g)   Protein (35 g)
Provides 119% of your daily iron needs based on a 2000-calorie diet.

RICE AND SPINACH PILAF

MAKES 4 SERVINGS

1 Tbsp (15 mL) coconut oil

3 Tbsp (45 mL) chopped onions

¾ cup (180 mL) brown basmati rice

⅔ cup (160 mL) vegetable stock

⅔ cup (160 mL) water

¼ cup (60 mL) white wine (or substitute more vegetable stock)

½–¾ tsp (2.5–4 mL) salt

2 Tbsp (30 mL/28 g) Skinny B cereal

⅓ cup (80 mL) coconut milk

2 Tbsp (30 mL) freshly grated Parmesan cheese

1 cup (250 mL) chopped baby spinach leaves

Sliced green onions (or fresh herbs), for garnish

Adding Holy Crap or Skinny B cereal to rice and other cooked side dishes is one of the easiest ways to make them more nutritious. It also makes them more filling. Serve this side dish with fish or chicken dishes like the Skinny B-Encrusted Salmon (page 100) or the Walnut-Crusted Chicken (page 113).

1. Heat the coconut oil in a heavy saucepan on medium heat. Add the onions and sauté until translucent. Stir in the rice and cook, stirring constantly, for about 5 minutes. Add the stock, water, wine and salt, mix well and bring to a rolling boil while stirring. Cover, reduce the heat to low and simmer for about 25 minutes, until all the water is absorbed. (Check the rice after 20 minutes, then every 5 minutes until it is done.)

2. Fold in the Skinny B cereal, coconut milk, cheese and spinach leaves. Remove from the heat and let sit for about 5 minutes.

3. Stir, spoon into a serving dish and garnish with green onions or herbs.

Tip: For a special Valentine's Day meal, mold the pilaf in a ramekin or heart-shaped dish before serving. Lightly coat a 4-oz (112-g) ramekin with coconut oil, fill it with the pilaf and invert onto a serving plate. Repeat for each serving.

This side dish is hearty and packed with fibre as well as good fats from the coconut milk.

NUTRITION FACTS: PER 96 G SERVING. Calories (150)   Total Fat (6 g) including Omega-3 (500 mg) and Omega-6 (415 mg)   Total Carbohydrates (21 g)   Dietary Fibre (2 g)   Protein (4 g)

SWEET POTATO KUGEL

MAKES 8 SERVINGS

A kugel is a sweet or savoury baked pudding made with noodles or potatoes. It is a staple side dish of Jewish holiday meals, but many people eat kugel for breakfast or lunch, or as a snack, too. This delicious version—a sweet potato kugel with apples—is adapted from a *New York Times* recipe and is a perfect accompaniment for chicken or beef brisket. Serve it straight from the oven or make it a day ahead and reheat it in a medium oven before serving.

Olive oil for oiling dish
½ cup (120 mL) water
¼ cup (60 mL/45 g) Holy Crap cereal + 1 tsp (4.5 g) for garnish
2 eggs
Salt to taste
2 large sweet potatoes (1¾–2 lb/800–900 g total), peeled and grated
2 slightly tart apples, peeled, cored and grated
1 Tbsp (15 mL) fresh lime juice
1 Tbsp (15 mL) honey or agave nectar
3–4 Tbsp (45–60 mL) melted unsalted butter (or margarine for kosher), divided, as needed

1. Heat the oven to 375F (190C). Lightly oil a 2-quart/2-L baking dish.
2. Pour the water into a bowl, stir in the Holy Crap cereal and let sit for 5 minutes. Set aside.
3. In a large bowl, beat the eggs with the salt. Add the soaked cereal, then the sweet potatoes and apples and mix until well combined. Stir in the lime juice.
4. In a small bowl, stir together the honey and 2 Tbsp (30 mL) of the melted butter (or margarine). Pour into the sweet potato mixture and combine well. Transfer the mixture to the baking dish, cover tightly with aluminum foil and bake for 45 minutes.
5. Remove the foil and brush the top of the kugel with melted butter (or margarine). Return to the oven and bake for another 15 to 20 minutes or longer, brushing every 5 minutes with butter (or margarine).

    The kugel is ready when the edges are browned, the top is browned in spots and the mixture is set. Remove from the heat and allow to cool for 10 to 15 minutes before serving. Garnish with a sprinkle of Holy Crap cereal.

NUTRITION FACTS: PER 150 G SERVING. Calories (150) Total Fat (7 g) including Omega-3 (625 mg) and Omega-6 (500 mg) Total Carbohydrates (23 g) Dietary Fibre (3 g) Protein (4 g)

QUINOA AND ZUCCHINI PILAF

MAKES 4–6 SERVINGS

1 cup (250 mL) quinoa

1½ cups (350 mL) water

2 Tbsp (30 mL) olive oil or coconut oil

½ cup (120 mL) chopped walnuts

¼ cup (60 mL) diced onions

2 medium zucchini, grated (or spiralized)

2 Tbsp (30 mL/28 g) Skinny B or Holy Crap cereal

½ tsp (2.5 mL) salt

¼ tsp (1 mL) freshly ground black pepper

Sprigs of parsley, for garnish

Tired of the same old rice or pasta side dishes? This quinoa and zucchini pilaf tastes like summer and, unlike most grains, quinoa is considered a complete protein as it contains all eight essential amino acids. Furthermore, it is high in fibre, a good source of protein, and very easy to digest. Try this pilaf warm with butter chicken, other curries or Walnut-Crusted Chicken (page 113), or as a stuffing for vegetables, or serve it on its own at room temperature for lunch.

1. In a saucepan, combine the quinoa and water and bring to a boil. Cover, reduce the heat to low and cook until all the water is absorbed, 12 to 15 minutes.
2. Heat the oil in a skillet on medium heat. Add the walnuts and cook for 2 to 3 minutes, being careful not to burn them. Add the onions and cook for 1 to 2 minutes more. Stir in the zucchini, Skinny B cereal, salt and pepper, stirring just until the zucchini is wilted, about 1 minute. Do not overcook, or it will become mushy. Remove from the heat.
3. Gently stir the cooked quinoa into the vegetable mixture until combined. Spoon into a serving dish and garnish with sprigs of parsley.

This recipe is a nutritious main or side dish that's high in fibre and a good source of protein.

NUTRITION FACTS: PER 182 G SERVING. Calories (300) Total Fat (20 g) including Omega-3 (500 mg) and Omega-6 (415 mg) Total Carbohydrates (25 g) Dietary Fibre (5 g) Protein (9 g)
Provides 18% of your daily vitamin C needs based on a 2000-calorie diet.

MARGHERITA PIZZA
MAKES ONE 8- TO 10-IN (20- TO 25-CM) PIZZA

2 eggs
1 cup (250 mL) cooked brown rice
½ cup (120 mL) cooked wild rice
2 Tbsp (30 mL/28 g) Skinny B cereal
2 Tbsp (30 mL) chopped onions
1 cup (250 mL) grated mozzarella cheese, divided in half
½ cup (120 mL) chopped grape tomatoes
3 Tbsp (45 mL) chopped basil

Sometimes fresh, simple and classic is best. And so it is with this delicious gluten-free pizza that highlights tomatoes, basil and cheese. Choose the best-quality ingredients you can find, including basil and tomatoes fresh from your garden or the farmers' market. (And, of course, feel free to change up the toppings to take advantage of whatever beautiful fresh produce you have on hand.) Serve this pizza as a main course or cut into smaller pieces as an appetizer.

1. Preheat the oven to 450F (230C). Line a pizza pan or baking sheet with parchment paper cut into an 8- to 10-in (20- to 25-cm) circle (depending on how thick you like the crust).

2. Beat the eggs in a large bowl, then add the cooked rice, Skinny B cereal, onions and ½ cup (120 mL) grated mozzarella cheese and mix until well combined. Spread this pizza base onto parchment paper circle placed on a pizza pan or baking sheet. Cook for approximately 20 minutes or until golden.

3. Top the pizza base with the remaining mozzarella and the grape tomatoes. Return to the oven and bake for another 8 to 10 minutes. Garnish with basil leaves, cut into 8 wedges and serve.

NUTRITION FACTS: PER 87 G SERVING (1 SLICE). Calories (150) Total Fat (7 g) including Omega–3 (250 mg) and Omega–6 (875 mg) Total Carbohydrates (10 g) Dietary Fibre (1 g) Protein (10 g)
Provides 23% of your daily calcium needs based on a 2000-calorie diet.

BEET AND KALE VEGGIE PATTIES
MAKES 12 PATTIES, EACH 3½ IN (9 CM) IN DIAMETER

Sweet beets and yams, as well as the cinnamon and dried fruit of Holy Crap Plus Gluten Free Oats, combine with savoury herbs for a festive patty evocative of a traditional Thanksgiving dinner—a vegetarian alternative to turkey with stuffing. If using vegan cheese, make sure to use a brand that melts well, or the patties may be crumbly.

2 Tbsp (30 mL) olive oil, divided in half
1 medium onion, finely chopped
2 cloves garlic, minced
3 leaves fresh sage, minced
1 sprig fresh thyme leaves, stems removed
1 small bunch kale, stems and ribs removed (about 3 loosely packed cups/710 mL)
1 cup (250 mL/140 g) Holy Crap Plus Gluten Free Oats
½ cup (120 mL) raw shelled sunflower seeds, soaked
1 small beet, peeled and grated (about 1 cup/250 mL)
1 small yam, peeled and grated (about 1 cup/250 mL)
1 cup (250 mL) grated mozzarella or cheddar cheese (dairy or vegan)
1 Tbsp (15 mL) gluten-free soy sauce
1 tsp (5 mL) black pepper
¼ cup (60 mL) tapioca flour
1 egg, beaten, or up to ½ cup (120 mL) Skinny B gel (page 20)
Cranberry sauce to serve (optional)

1. Line a large baking tray with parchment paper and coat with 1 Tbsp (15 mL) olive oil.
2. Heat the remaining olive oil in a skillet over medium-high heat. Add the onions, garlic and herbs and sauté until the onions are translucent. Transfer the onion mixture to a large bowl to cool.
3. Add the kale to the hot skillet, add a splash of water and cover with lid. Cook over medium heat for 1 minute or until the kale is wilted. Allow to cool and squeeze out liquid.
4. Place the wilted kale, Holy Crap Plus Gluten Free Oats and drained sunflower seeds in the bowl of a food processor and pulse until all the ingredients are well incorporated.
5. Add the kale mixture, grated beets and yams, cheese, soy sauce and pepper to the cooked onions and toss well. Add tapioca flour and toss ingredients to coat. Stir in the egg. If using Skinny B gel as an egg substitute, add it a bit at a time and just use enough so that mixture holds its shape but isn't wet (you might not need all the gel).
6. Preheat the oven to 400F (205C). To shape the patties, use a ring mold (or the lid of a canning jar) and gently the press mixture into rounds on the baking tray. Bake for 12 minutes, then flip the patties and cook until the edges are crispy, about 10 to 15 minutes more.
7. Serve warm with a spoonful of cranberry sauce.

SOUTHWEST VEGGIE BURGER

For a spicy patty more suited to the usual burger fixin's, replace the sage and thyme with ½ tsp (2.5 mL) each cumin and chili flakes; replace the beet with ½ cup (120 mL) each corn kernels and cooked black beans; swap out the Holy Crap Plus Gluten Free Oats for ¼ cup (60 mL/56 g) Skinny B plus 1 cup (250 mL) cooked quinoa or brown rice. Top with sliced avocado or eat on a bun with "the works."

Tip: Okay, we admit it, this recipe is more labour intensive than store-bought veggie patties (which are convenient but not as delicious). But these patties freeze well: separate them with layers of parchment paper before freezing. Why not make a double batch and bring them out as needed for quick weeknight dinners? Reheat in the oven or a lightly oiled skillet.

NUTRITION FACTS: PER 100 G SERVING (1 PATTY). Calories (210)   Total Fat (10 g) including Omega-3 (0.25 g) and Omega-6 (1 g)   Total Carbohydrates (20 g)   Dietary Fibre (5 g)   Protein (10 g) *Provides 65% of your daily vitamin A needs and 45% of your daily vitamin C needs based on a 2000-calorie diet.*

WALNUT-CRUSTED CHICKEN
MAKES 4 SERVINGS

Forget Shake 'n Bake! Try this spicy, nutty, crunchy chicken instead. Marinated in chipotle and garlic, coated with Skinny B and walnuts, and baked rather than fried, it's a perfect protein to add to a summer salad or to take to the beach as part of a picnic. Thanks to Charlene SanJenko of PowHERhouse, a former personal trainer and now a vibrant social entrepreneur who embodies lifestyle with leadership, for contributing this recipe. Remember to start this dish the day before you plan to serve it, as the chicken needs to marinate for several hours or overnight. And seek out the best-quality organic free-range chicken you can find—you will taste the difference.

MARINATED CHICKEN

1½ tsp (7.5 mL) canned chipotle peppers in adobo sauce
½ tsp (2.5 mL) crushed garlic
Bragg's liquid soy seasoning
Chipotle pepper (or black pepper)
2 skinless, boneless whole chicken breasts, cut in half

1. In a small bowl, combine the canned chipotle peppers and sauce and the garlic. Season to taste with Bragg's and dry chipotle pepper.
2. Place the chicken breasts in a large resealable bag or in a baking dish. Add the marinade, ensuring that the chicken pieces are well coated. Refrigerate for a couple of hours or overnight, turning the chicken a couple of times so it gets evenly marinated.

PEANUT BUTTER AND MISO SAUCE

1 Tbsp (15 mL) peanut butter
1½ tsp (7.5 mL) miso paste
1 Tbsp (15 mL) sesame oil
1 Tbsp (15 mL) Bragg's liquid soy seasoning
1 Tbsp (15 mL) balsamic vinegar

1. In a small bowl or a blender, combine all the ingredients until well mixed. Slowly add water until the dressing reaches your preferred consistency. (We like it thick enough to coat a fork without dripping.)

CONTINUED ON NEXT PAGE

CRISPY COATING

Coconut oil

⅓ cup (80 mL) walnut pieces, crushed in a food processor

3 Tbsp (45 mL/42 g) Skinny B cereal

½ tsp (2.5 mL) garlic powder

Chipotle pepper (or black pepper) to taste

1 Tbsp (15 mL) brown sugar

Salt

1. Preheat the oven to 375F (190C). Grease a baking sheet with a thin layer of coconut oil.

2. Place all the ingredients in a bowl and mix until well combined. Transfer the coating to a pie plate or a large shallow bowl.

3. Dredge the chicken in the coating mix, being sure to cover both sides completely and evenly, and carefully place the pieces on the baking sheet. Bake for 15 to 20 minutes per side, checking occasionally to be sure it's browning well but not burning.

4. For a crispier crust, turn on your broiler and broil the chicken for the final 2 minutes. Serve warm or at room temperature, on a platter or on individual plates. Drizzle with some of the peanut butter and miso sauce.

NUTRITION FACTS: PER 100 G SERVING (½ CHICKEN BREAST). Calories (260) Total Fat (14 g) including Omega-3 (1.5 g) and Omega-6 (1 g) Total Carbohydrates (8 g) Dietary Fibre (3 g) Protein (26 g) *Provides 14% of your daily total iron needs based on a 2000-calorie diet.*

NAUGHTY BUT NICE SWEETS

I believe in making healthy choices most of the time and occasionally indulging in decadent treats. Two big secrets to health are eating whole foods and eating in moderation. The same rules apply with sweets. Homemade treats taste better than store-bought ones and allow you to avoid additives, select natural fats and sugars, and sneak in healthy ingredients like our cereals. Serve these sweets in small portions and savour.

HOLY CRAP DARK CHOCOLATE BARK

MAKES 20 PIECES

12 oz (336 g) vegan semi-
  sweet chocolate chips
2 Tbsp (30 mL/28 g) Holy Crap
  cereal
1 cup (250 mL) chopped
  walnuts
½ cup (120 mL) dried tart
  cherries
¼ cup (60 mL) raw unsalted
  pumpkin seeds
Pinch of sea salt

These rich, dark, rustic pieces of handmade love will satisfy your chocolate craving, and they're easy to make. Double or triple the recipe to make gifts for all your friends and neighbours.

1. Line a rimmed baking sheet with parchment paper.
2. In a double boiler, melt the chocolate chips on low heat. Stir the melted chocolate for a couple of minutes until it becomes glossy and starts to cool, then pour it onto the baking sheet in a square shape of even thickness.
3. Sprinkle evenly with Holy Crap cereal, walnuts, cherries, pumpkin seeds and a pinch of sea salt. Allow to cool completely.
4. Remove and discard the parchment paper, then break the solid chocolate bark into 20 even pieces and store in an airtight container in the fridge for up to 1 week.

Tip: If you don't have a double boiler, set a stainless steel bowl inside a metal colander and place the colander over a saucepan of water on low heat, making sure the bottom of the colander doesn't touch the water.

NUTRITION FACTS: PER 28 G SERVING (1 PIECE). Calories (140) Total Fat (11 g) including Omega-3 (0.5 g) and Omega-6 (0.5 g) Total Carbohydrates (11 g) Dietary Fibre (2 g) Protein (3 g)
Provides 9% of your daily iron needs based on a 2000-calorie diet.

HAZELNUT CHOCOLATE TRUFFLES

MAKES 24 TRUFFLES

½ cup (120 mL) water
2 Tbsp (30 mL/28 g) Holy Crap
  or Skinny B cereal
1¼ cups (300 mL) hazelnuts (or
  other nuts)
1¼ cups (300 mL) Medjool
  dates, pitted
2 tsp (10 mL) vanilla extract
3½ Tbsp (50 mL) cocoa powder
¼ tsp (1 mL) salt
¾ cup (180 mL) shredded
  coconut (or finely chopped
  nuts)

These decadent little chocolate truffles, which are free of gluten, dairy and refined sugar, will please adults and children alike, including the fussiest members of your family. They are also suitable for grain-free, Paleo and vegan diets. And they can be made in just a few minutes. The combination of ground dates and nuts makes a great "dough" that is fun to work with and offers so much more nutrition than store-bought truffles. Thank you to Lisa Cantkier, holistic nutritionist and founder of GlutenFreeFind.com, for contributing this recipe.

1. Pour the water into a bowl, stir in the Holy Crap or Skinny B cereal and let sit for 5 minutes. Set aside.
2. Grind the hazelnuts in a food processor, then add the dates and grind again until you have a smooth consistency. Transfer the mixture to a large bowl and add the vanilla, cocoa powder, salt and soaked cereal. Stir until well combined.
3. Place the shredded coconut in a shallow bowl.
4. Shape the truffles by scooping a tablespoonful of the hazelnut mixture into your hands and rolling it between your hands to form a ball. Roll the ball in the coconut and set aside. Repeat with the remaining hazelnut mixture.
5. Transfer the truffles to an airtight container and refrigerate until ready to eat (up to 1 week). They'll soften quickly at room temperature.

NUTRITION FACTS: PER 30 G SERVING (1 TRUFFLE). Calories (140) Total Fat (10 g) including Omega-3 (75 mg) and Omega-6 (60 mg) Total Carbohydrates (13 g) Dietary Fibre (3 g) Protein (3 g)
Provides 11% of your daily iron needs based on a 2000-calorie diet.

CHOCOLATE TRUFFLES

MAKES 50 TRUFFLES

2 cups (475 mL) vegan semi-
sweet chocolate chips (buy
the best quality you can)
¾ cup (180 mL) coconut milk
1 tsp (5 mL) vanilla extract
½–¾ tsp (2.5–4 mL) salt
1 cup (250 mL/185 g) Skinny B
or Holy Crap cereal
Cocoa powder for rolling (use
coconut or finely chopped
nuts for variations)

Chocolate truffles are named for their shape, which is said to resemble the highly prized fruit of the Tuber fungus. But the similarities end there. These creamy, rich sweets are perfect with a cup of coffee or a glass of port. Allow them to soften slightly before serving.

1. In a double boiler, melt the chocolate chips on low heat, stirring frequently. Stir the coconut milk into the melted chocolate until smooth, then stir in the vanilla and salt. Remove from the heat and stir in the cereal. Refrigerate for at least an hour (or overnight).
2. Place the cocoa in a shallow bowl. (If you are making several variations, place the coconut and nuts in their own individual bowls.)
3. Shape the truffles by scooping a teaspoonful of the chocolate mixture into your hands and rolling it between your hands to form a ball. Roll the ball in the cocoa powder and set aside. Repeat with the remaining chocolate mixture.
4. Transfer the truffles to an airtight container and refrigerate for up to 1 week. Let them come to room temperature before serving.

 Tip: If you don't have a double boiler, set a stainless steel bowl inside a metal colander and place the colander over a saucepan of water on low heat, making sure the bottom of the colander doesn't touch the water.

NUTRITION FACTS: PER 15 G SERVING (1 TRUFFLE). Calories (70)   Total Fat (3 g)   Total Carbohydrates (7 g)   Dietary Fibre (2 g)   Protein (3 g)

Cuckoo for Coconut

Don't be put off by the high fat and high calorie content of coconut products. They are highly beneficial to the body. The fat in coconut is different from the fat we store in our body, as it's made up of medium-chain triglycerides (MCTs) that are very easy for the body to break down and use as energy. In other words, they can actually boost your metabolism and help you to lose weight!

Although coconut does contain a lot of saturated fat, it is completely different from the saturated fat found in foods of animal origin. Unrefined plant-based saturated fat from coconuts and extra-virgin coconut oil is always free of cholesterol. Coconut fat is also great for cooking because it doesn't oxidize with heat, as many liquid vegetable oils do.

And coconut milks are a great alternative to dairy. They are creamy and rich tasting but contain no lactose or cholesterol. Coconut water is also full of nutrients that help to hydrate the body.

COCONUT RICE PUDDING

MAKES 5–6 SERVINGS

½ cup (120 mL) water

2 Tbsp (30 mL/28 g) Holy Crap cereal

¼ cup (60 mL) arborio rice

1 can (13.5 fl oz/400 mL) coconut milk

Orange zest

2 Tbsp (30 mL) honey, maple syrup or sugar

Ribbons of fresh coconut, for garnish

Orange peel, cut in ribbons, for garnish

A favorite winter dessert around our house is this creamy coconut rice pudding. It's a healthier, and tastier version, of a classic rice pudding. I like how the tang of the orange peel balances its heartiness. If it's just Brian and I we'll serve it in a small ramekin. For company, it's easily dressed up in a martini glass with a garnish.

1. Preheat the oven to 250F (120C). Have ready an 8-in (20-cm) square baking pan.
2. Pour the water into a bowl, stir in the Holy Crap cereal and let sit for 5 minutes. Stir in the remaining ingredients, except the garnishes, then pour into the baking pan and bake for about 45 minutes. Stir gently and bake for another 45 minutes.
3. Spoon into individual bowls and garnish with ribbons of fresh coconut and orange peel. Leftovers will keep refrigerated in an airtight container for a couple of days.

NUTRITION FACTS: PER 115 G SERVING. Calories (270)   Total Fat (15 g) including Omega-3 (750 mg) and Omega-6 (625 mg)   Total Carbohydrates (25 g)   Dietary Fibre (2 g)   Protein (5 g)

MINI CHOCOLATE CHEESECAKES

MAKES 8 SERVINGS

8 gluten-free "Oreo-style" cookies

8 oz (226 g) regular cream cheese (do not use whipped)

¼ cup (60 mL) white sugar

1 egg

2 tsp (10 mL) vanilla extract

¼ cup (60 mL) plain non-fat Greek yogurt

1 Tbsp (15 mL/14 g) Skinny B cereal

8 fresh raspberries, for garnish

I ate very well growing up. My mother, who was an excellent cook, began each meal with a soup, followed up with a main course of coq au vin or something similar and ended with a cheese course. Sweets were rare in our house—until we moved to Canada. Here, I discovered my love of chocolate. These decadent mini cheesecakes—inspired by Annie at the Sweet Frosting blog—indulge my taste for chocolate without going overboard on the fat and sugar.

1. Preheat the oven to 350F (175C). Line an 8-cup muffin tin with paper liners.
2. Separate cookies and place one half in each liner, icing side up. Roughly chop up and reserve un-iced halves.
3. Place the cream cheese and sugar in a bowl. Beat with an electric hand mixer until well combined, then add egg and vanilla and beat until smooth, scraping down the sides. Fold in yogurt and cereal, making sure they are well distributed. Let sit for 5 minutes, then fold in cookie pieces.
4. Pour the batter into the muffin tins and bake for 18 minutes. Remove from oven and allow to cool to room temperature without removing from the muffin tin. Then transfer to a plate and refrigerate for at least 4 hours before serving.
5. To serve, soften at room temperature for 15 minutes, then peel off the paper liners and garnish with fresh raspberries. Leftovers will keep refrigerated in an airtight container for 2 to 3 days.

Looking to make big changes in your overall health? Start by making small changes like adding Holy Crap or Skinny B to your favourite indulgences.

NUTRITION FACTS: PER 66 G SERVING. Calories (220) Total Fat (13 g) including Omega-3 (190 mg) and Omega-6 (155 mg) Total Carbohydrates (19 g) Dietary Fibre (1 g) Protein (4 g)

DENSE CHOCOLATE CAKE

MAKES 12 SERVINGS

¼ cup (60 mL) water

2 Tbsp (30 mL/28 g) Skinny B cereal

1 can (19 oz/540 g) black beans, drained and rinsed

2 large eggs

½ cup (120 mL) sugar (coconut sugar, brown sugar or white sugar)

3 Tbsp (45 mL) cocoa powder

1 tsp (5 mL) pure vanilla extract

1 tsp (5 mL) baking powder

Zest from 1 orange

½–¾ tsp (2.5–4 mL) salt

½ cup (120 mL) chopped vegan chocolate

1 cup (250 mL) fresh blackberries, for garnish

This dense, fudgy cake is a breeze to make, and you can easily dress it up for special occasions. Don't expect a sweet cake, however; its slightly bitter dark-chocolate flavour pairs well with the similarly bitter orange zest. For a special Valentine's Day dessert, cut individual slices of cake, then use a cookie cutter to form small heart-shaped cakes that you can garnish with a fruit coulis and fresh berries.

1. Preheat the oven to 350F (175C) and line a loaf pan with parchment paper.
2. Pour the water into a bowl, stir in the Skinny B cereal and let sit for 5 minutes.
3. Place all the ingredients, except the chopped chocolate and blackberries, in a blender and process until smooth. Pour the batter into the loaf pan, sprinkle the chopped chocolate evenly across the surface and use the back of a spoon to push it all into the batter. Bake for 35 minutes.
4. Remove from the oven and transfer the loaf pan to a wire rack to cool completely. To serve, remove the cake from the pan, discard the parchment paper and cut into individual slices. Garnish with fresh blackberries. The cake will keep refrigerated in an airtight container for 5 days.

Talk about a cake with benefits! It's packed with protein and fibre to satisfy your taste buds and your body. And using coconut sugar, which is mineral rich and lower on the glycemic index, is an amazing alternative to conventional sugar.

NUTRITION FACTS: PER 56 G SERVING. Calories (100) Total Fat (4 g) including Omega-3 (230 mg) and Omega-6 (190 mg) Total Carbohydrates (17 g) Dietary Fibre (3 g) Protein (4 g)
Provides 12% of your daily iron needs based on a 2000-calorie diet.

PEACH CRUMBLE

MAKES 8 SERVINGS

Butter for greasing pan
1 cup (250 mL/140 g) Holy Crap Plus Gluten Free Oats
½ cup (120 mL) roughly chopped walnuts
¼ cup (60 mL) brown sugar
Pinch of salt
¼ cup (60 mL) cold butter
4–5 medium peaches, peeled and sliced

Crumble is a quintessential comfort food; it's easy to make, endlessly versatile and very forgiving. And it complements just about any fruit you can think of. I often make crumble when I get a last-minute invitation to a potluck or when friends drop by for dinner. Serve this crumble with good-quality vanilla ice cream (or vanilla non-dairy frozen dessert) or with dollops of whipped cream, crème fraîche or plain non-fat Greek yogurt.

1. Preheat the oven to 350F (175C). Lightly butter a 9-in (23-cm) square pan.
2. In a large bowl, whisk together the Holy Crap Plus Gluten Free Oats, walnuts, brown sugar and salt. Using a pastry blender or a fork, cut in the cold butter until the mixture resembles peas. Set aside.
3. Layer the peaches in the bottom of the pan, making sure to cover the entire surface, including the corners. Pour the crumble mixture over the peaches and smooth it out, ensuring you cover the peaches entirely. Bake for 30 to 35 minutes.
4. Remove the crumble from the oven, spoon into individual bowls and serve warm. Leftover crumble will keep refrigerated in an airtight container for several days.

NUTRITION FACTS: PER 100 G SERVING. Calories (330) Total Fat (18 g) including Omega-3 (0.5 g) and Omega-6 (1.5 g) Total Carbohydrates (40 g) Dietary Fibre (5 g) Protein (7 g).
Provides 67% of your daily vitamin C needs based on a 2000-calorie diet.

ENDNOTES

1   Diana Allen, MS CNS, *Chia Seed* (Salt Lake City: Woodland Publishing, 2010).

2   Chia Seeds Nutrition Profile, nutritiondata.self.com. For more information see "The importance of the omega-6/omega-3 fatty acid ratio in cardio-vascular disease and other chronic diseases" by Artemis P. Simopoulos on Pubmed.gov (http://www.ncbi.nlm.nih.gov/pubmed/18408140). See also MedlinePlus (nlm.nig.gov/medlinplus/) and medicalnewstoday.com for articles on chia seeds.

3   Buckwheat Nutrition Facts, nutritiondata.self.com.

4   Hemp Seeds Nutrition Facts, see nutritiondata.self.com. See also authori-tynutrition.com, mercola.com and medicalnewstoday.com for their articles on the health benefits of hemp.

5   Noah Scovronick, "Reducing global health risks through mitigation of short-lived climate pollutants," World Health Organization scoping report for policy makers (2015). Available at http://www.who.int/.

ACKNOWLEDGEMENTS

Many thanks to my co-author Claudia Howard, who tested, tasted and tweaked the recipes. I'm especially appreciative of your unflagging enthusiasm from start to finish in managing all the details involved in cooking up a cookbook. I would also like to extend my gratitude to the following people:

To Carol Pope, for your assistance in helping us to tell the Holy Crap story.

To everyone at Douglas & McIntyre for taking on *The Holy Crap Cookbook*, including managing editor Anna Comfort O'Keeffe, who championed the cookbook and provided masterful direction as well as three delicious recipes. We are grateful for the expertise and thoughtful guidance of editors Lucy Kenward, Arlene Prunkl and Shirarose Wilensky as well as editorial assistant Tori Hannesson. Thank you to ace book designer Diane Robertson for the lovely pages. Many thanks to Marisa Alps and her marketing and publicity team for helping to get the word out. Everyone's support and skill is much appreciated.

To Christina Symons, for her masterful food styling and magnificent photography that always creates a visual feast. And I'm especially grateful to Christina for connecting us with the good people at Douglas & McIntyre.

To our graphic designer Karen Weissenborn for creating the Holy Crap logo and product packaging and to digital designer Blair Massey.

To nutritionist Erika Weissenborn for reviewing the nutritional information of the recipes and providing the nutrition insights that appear throughout the book.

To everyone who generously shared their recipes in this book, including Kathy Smart, Lisa Cantkier, Charlene SanJenko, Guy Mitchell, Annie Wu, Lori Pepper and Leo Tabibzadegan.

To *Dragons' Den* executive producer Tracie Tighe, producer Molly Middleton and Dragon Jim Treliving.

To everyone at the Opportunity Fund, Aspire Self Employment Program and the Sunshine Coast Credit Union.

To Christopher Meyer, Watson Goepel, John Smiley and Wolridge Mahon.

To the HapiFoods Group employees, my wholehearted thanks for everything you do and the soul you put into every bag of cereal.

To my husband, partner and Holy Crap co-founder Brian, thank you for this amazing journey we're on.

And last, but definitely not least, Brian and I are incredibly grateful to all our customers. Your stories inspire us.

INDEX

Page numbers in **bold** refer to photos.

ABOUT THE CONTRIBUTORS

Author **Corin Mullins** is the CEO and co-founder of HapiFoods Group Inc. (2009) and creator of Holy Crap cereal, which has grown in a few short years to an award-winning business success story. She was named an EY Entrepreneurial Winning Women in 2013 and, in 2012, was ranked 14 among Canada's top female entrepreneurs by PROFIT/*Chatelaine*. She lives in Sechelt, BC, with her husband Brian.

Co-author **Claudia Howard** is a communications professional working as the vice-president of marketing at HapiFoods Group Inc. (2009). She is passionate about developing healthy recipes with local ingredients. She divides her time between Gibsons, BC, and Palm Springs, CA.

Holistic nutritionist **Erika Weissenborn** has a Bachelor of Science in Food Nutrition and Health and, as a Certified Nutritional Practitioner, studies both science-based and holistic nutrition and orthomolecular health. She teaches at the Institute of Holistic Nutrition, Capilano University and the University of British Columbia. Her notes on healthy eating are located above the nutrition facts throughout the recipe section of this book. She lives in Vancouver, BC.

Photographer **Christina Symons** specializes in food, garden and lifestyle topics. She has contributed to numerous books and publications including the *Vancouver Sun*, *Globe & Mail* and *Style at Home*, as well as co-authoring two books with Harbour Publishing, *Everyday Eden* and *Sow Simple* (2012). She lives in Sechelt, BC.

JOHN HUDDART PHOTO